The Dad Report

**This Large Print Book carries the
Seal of Approval of N.A.V.H.**

The Dad
★ Report ★

FATHERS, SONS, *and* BASEBALL FAMILIES

KEVIN COOK

CENTER POINT LARGE PRINT
THORNDIKE, MAINE

This Center Point Large Print edition
is published in the year 2015 by arrangement with
W. W. Norton & Company, Inc.

The text of this Large Print edition is unabridged.
In other aspects, this book may vary
from the original edition.
Printed in the United States of America
on permanent paper.
Set in 16-point Times New Roman type.

ISBN: 978-1-62899-719-4

Publisher's Cataloging-In-Publication Data
(Prepared by The Donohue Group, Inc.)

Cook, Kevin, 1956–
   The Dad Report : fathers, sons, and baseball families / Kevin Cook. —
Center Point Large Print edition.
      pages ; cm
   Includes bibliographical references.
   ISBN: 978-1-62899-719-4 (library binding : alk. paper)
   "An award-winning sportswriter's inside look at how baseball
         families share our national pastime"—Provided by publisher.
   1. Baseball—Anecdotes. 2. Fathers and sons—Anecdotes.
      3. Baseball players—Family relationships—United States.
      4. Large type books. I. Title.
GV873 .C68 2015b
796.35—dc23

To Lily and Cal,
whose dad I'm glad to be

CONTENTS

The Dad Report

PROLOGUE
★ *He Calls His Shot* ★

He came up to bat against the best kid pitcher in the neighborhood: me. He was heavy but not fat, at least not fat all over. His face and belly had widened over the years, getting rounder the way aging athletes' faces and bellies tend to do, but his arms and legs were bulky with muscle and his pigeon-toed gait was as balanced as a dancer's. If you've ever seen flickery black-and-white film of Babe Ruth, you've seen that walk. Like Ruth, my dad was light on his feet.

He stepped to the plate with his usual good-humored swagger, nodding to the pitcher as if to say hello.

Nodding to me.

In that summer of 1969, I was truly my father's son. A Little League all-star, the starting pitcher in our annual father-son game. "Warren Township's preteen phenom," a local newspaper called me, "with an earned run average of 0.20."

I had no trouble with the other fathers. They saw themselves as ballplayers despite the fact that they had never played high school baseball, much less college or pro ball. Few could hit a fungo without whiffing. Showboating at the plate in the father-son game, they all swung too hard at my 65-mile-an-hour fastballs. One literally shut his eyes as he swung. I struck him out. Others topped grounders to my infielders, who grinned while firing to first for easy outs.

But my dad was different. For one thing, he was older than the others—forty-three years old the year I turned twelve. He was heavier than most of them, too, his 210 pounds distributed unevenly on a five-foot-nine frame. More important, he was better. He moved with a smooth economy that made the other dads look clumsy. Not that they could see it. To them, he was the grizzled fat guy who watched Little League games from his car and never offered advice. That's why he'd spent most of this father-son game on the bench, watching the other dads try to run to first without tripping over their feet. He never mentioned that he'd been a pro, a minor-league star once celebrated with fireworks on "Art Cook Night" in Kingston, Ontario.

He stretched, getting limber, twirling his bat like Willie Stargell. I waited, rubbing the ball up. Finally he reached out, pointing his bat at the right-field fence to say, *That's where the ball's going*. Calling his shot, like Ruth.

I threw him my best fastball. His swing was quick, a smooth weight shift, thick wrists snapping the bat through the strike zone to a sound I can still hear half a century later. A *crack* like a hammer on a seashell. Goodbye.

The ball was still rising as it cleared the fence. It reached its zenith as Dad dropped his bat and began trotting toward first base. I dropped my glove and ran home. Not to home plate—all the way home.

I locked myself in my room, trying not to cry. Before long, I heard my parents arguing. My mother was angry. "How *could* you?"

Dad sounded puzzled. "What am I supposed to do?" he said. "Strike out on purpose?"

I was mad at both of us—mad at him for showing me up, and, more than anything else, mad at myself for failing at the game we shared.

Today, looking back at a meaningless father-son ballgame forty-five years ago, I'm surprised at how vivid that day was. *Is.* Maybe that's because it was the day I began to realize I would never be half the ballplayer he was.

Instead, I wound up as a writer—sports, mostly—and stayed close to baseball. Over the years, I spent time with players in major-league ballparks as well as dugouts, hotels, cars, palatial homes, golf courses, bars and restaurants, even a strip club. Some of the players were stars, some were scrubs, and many of them enjoyed talking about their fathers. Those conversations led to this book. They led me to believe that there's something special about the way families share the game. It's not always the same way, but there are patterns. Buddy Bell and Cal Ripken Jr. wanted to be just like their dads. Barry Bonds and Ken Griffey Jr. wanted to outdo theirs. Three generations of Daniel Boone's descendants—Ray, Bob, and Bob's sons Bret and Aaron, all of them All-Stars—spent half a century one-upping each other, and they're still at it. And that's just a few of the major-league families you'll meet in these pages. There are thousands of other families sharing the game in their own ways, including countless fathers and sons who have a hard time talking about much of anything *except* baseball. I've heard many variations on that theme:

"My dad never said much, but he liked telling me about Ted Williams and Mickey Mantle."

"I had nothing in common with my grandpa, but we could always talk baseball."

"My father was a drunk. The only good times we had were watching ballgames on TV."

"If not for baseball, I don't know if we would have said much at all."

Dad and I were like that. We didn't talk much for years. What was there to say? We weren't about to discuss our feelings, our health, politics, or religion. In time, though, we would learn (or relearn) that we could always talk baseball. "Randy Johnson 15 Ks!" can be another way to say hello. We wound up talking on the phone almost every night, almost always about base-ball. We talked baseball as a way of talking about everything else, and we named our nightly call the Dad Report.

Maybe all this says something about American manhood. Maybe the tight-lipped baseball hero— Gary Cooper playing Lou Gehrig in *Pride of the Yankees*; Joe DiMaggio rounding the bases, expressionless; Curt Schilling helping the Red Sox win a World Series while a transplanted tendon bled through his sock—isn't the best role model. Maybe men should open up more, spill our guts, and talk about our feelings instead of runs, hits, and errors. I don't know about that. Maybe it's true. What I know is that Dad and I shared baseball more than anything else. I can tell you that he never mentioned religion except to say that God had to be a baseball fan, because the Bible starts, "In the big inning . . ."

On the day he homered off me and I ran home, I heard him arguing with my mother. Later, he tapped on my door. I wouldn't open it. I didn't feel like talking. He probably didn't, either, but he tapped the door again. I didn't answer. Finally, he apologized in the only way he knew how. He slipped a wordless apology under the door: a five-dollar bill.

1
★ *Golden Boy* ★
ART COOK, BEGINNINGS

Art Cook was a left-hander who pitched in the minor leagues in the 1940s and '50s. I knew a few details about his career. Long before his father-son home run off me, he gave up a tape-measure shot of his own, a homer off the bat of Indiana University slugger Ted Kluszewski, who went on to an All-Star career with the Cincinnati Reds. Dad always claimed that the ball Big Klu hit off him was still in the air. He said there were radar reports that it bounced off *Sputnik.*

He liked to tell stories like that. How a minor-league team once honored him for a 20-win season, presenting him with a gold watch before the last game of the season, and then he got shelled in the third inning. "They wanted their watch back," he said. Or how he broke the little finger on his left hand: a screwball didn't screw, and the ball came back at him twice as fast as he threw it, smashing the pinkie on his pitching hand. The meat hand, he called it, as opposed to the glove hand. That finger was crooked for the rest of his life, so bendy that he could tug it backward until the nail touched the back of his hand. I always liked that trick. It was only years later that I asked him what happened right after that pinkie-smashing line drive. He said he fielded the ball, threw the batter out, and finished the inning. It sounded like a tall tale.

I was almost thirty when I started finding out who Art Cook was before he was my dad. Not just a middle school coach and night school librarian, not just a broke gambler sitting alone in his car. In his time, he was a hero, the kind of guy teammates hoist on their shoulders and carry off the field. His tall tales were true.

Arthur Bruce Cook was born in an Indiana farmhouse in the spring of 1925. It was the year Al Capone took over the bootlegging rackets in Chicago. It was the year of the Monkey Trial, when Dayton, Tennessee, schoolteacher John Scopes got jailed for teaching Darwin's theory of evolution. Indiana always seemed to be sand-wiched between things that mattered. That spring, a tornado tore eastward across Missouri and Illinois. The Tri-State Twister, one of the deadliest on record, knocked silos and farmhouses off their foundations, its 300 mph winds sending Model Ts flitting through the air. The tornado stripped the bark off trees. It turned cornstalks and bits of straw into missiles that impaled telephone poles and unlucky livestock, and killed more than a thousand Midwesterners on its way toward Ed Cook's farm.

Ed and his pregnant wife, Ella, gathered their four children (Robert was ten years old, Wilbur seven, Charles four, and Wilma two) in the dirt-walled storm cellar, where Ella lay on a straw mattress, squeezing her children's hands. While the wind howled overhead, she prayed that the storm and her distress wouldn't harm the baby in her belly. Three months later, she gave birth to a fourth son. The Cooks named him Arthur Bruce so that his initials would lead off the alphabet.

He was their golden boy, a towhead in a brown-haired family. Young Arthur had an easygoing disposition from the get-go. Despite growing up in the middle of the Great Depression, he had what the Cooks described as a smooth row to hoe. His siblings helped him do his chores. Soon he was throwing a ball with his brothers, stinging their hands through the papery leather of their mitts as he progressed from sandlot runt to schoolboy phenom. At the age of fifteen, he was facing college and semipro hitters in local all-star games. He'd zip a fastball under a cleanup hitter's hands, then fool him with a changeup. The boy the *Indianapolis Star* called "Art Cook of Rural Route 8, most valuable member of the recent Junior Baseball tournament," was signing autographs before he turned seventeen.

By then his father, a longtime smoker, was weak

with lung cancer. Ed Cook died at home, sitting in his favorite chair with his family around him. Death seemed less alien in those days, particularly to farm people, but Art clung to the memory of his father's last breath, the life going out of him like air out of a balloon. Art sent a poem to the high school newspaper as a tribute to his father. "From shining dawn till the sun's last ray, we teach ourselves and our sons to play," he wrote. It was basketball season, so he pictured "the moisture on his furrowed brow as father tried to teach Junior how to pass and cut and block and fade." He concluded, "There's a thrill in the huddle with coach and boys, and a thrill in the crowd and its deafening noise. But the greatest thrill to a high school lad is a 'Nice game, son,' and a 'Thank you, Dad.'"

While still a high schooler, Art tossed a no-hitter in a 1943 amateur tournament. Many of the other players were in their twenties. Another Hoosier schoolboy star, future Dodger Gil Hodges, played in the same event. There were thousands of phenoms like them scattered across America, each one a prince of his realm. In that pre-TV era, the only way for most Americans to see big-league baseball was to drive for hours on two-lane state roads to a city like St. Louis or Chicago, and that was a special occasion. If you were a baseball fan living outside the big cities, you spent most of the summer following the local amateur and minor-league clubs, whose stars might loom as large in your mind as Joe DiMaggio and Ted Williams. Not even the Yankees on New York's WINS radio or the Cardinals on KMOX reached more than a patch of the country, but your hometown nine was on the radio day after day. (Or night after night. Minor-league teams experimented with night baseball in trial-and-error fashion, using portable lights that left blind spots where outfielders went to their hands and knees to find the ball—lights that sometimes exploded in a show of midgame fireworks.) Morning papers in Tulsa, Birmingham, Bakersfield, Paducah, and scores of other towns gave the local heroes more ink than big-league pennant races. On Art Cook's eighteenth birthday in 1943, there were more than four hundred teams in fifty-five minor leagues across the U.S. By the end of the '40s there were fifty-nine minor leagues, a total that would shrink to only fifteen by 1963, when TV's *Game of the Week* brought major-league ball into homes from coast to coast. The twenty-first century has seen a bush-league renaissance as fans rediscover the pleasures of seven-dollar tickets and dollar hot dogs, but the mid-twentieth century was the true heyday of minor-league baseball.

Branch Rickey, the Brooklyn Dodgers' general manager, attended the 1943 Junior Baseball tournament in Indianapolis. Rickey promptly signed Gil Hodges, but it was Art Cook who won a trip to the World Series as the tournament's best player. Before boarding a bus to St. Louis, he flashed a cocky grin for an *Indianapolis Star* photographer. The caption called him "a 145-pound, five-foot nine-inch, blond left-hander who mixes a nice curve with a fast ball."

The blond lefty remembered that World Series as much for the ballpark as for the games. Sportsman's Park in St. Louis was a palace, with infield grass like a putting green and dirt raked so smooth there wasn't a pebble on it. Most of all, he remembered the outfield dimensions. Sitting near the home dugout, within shouting distance of Commissioner Kenesaw Mountain Landis, Art was thinking of how he'd pitch at Sportsman's Park when he got to the majors.

"It was 426 feet to center," he said forty years later, "but only 310 down the right-field line," where the Cardinals' left-handed Stan Musial aimed. "So you pitch to the park."

"Meaning what?" I asked.

"Meaning have an idea. You think about the hitter, the wind, how you're throwing that day. A right-hander with power in a park like that, you might stay up and away. He wants to pull the ball. Let him hit one four hundred feet for an out."

"What about Musial?"

Dad said, "Walk him."

The Yankees thumped Musial and the Cardinals in the 1943 World Series. Art Cook returned to

Indianapolis, where he accepted an athletic scholarship to Butler University. Too young to fight in World War II, he pitched for Butler's baseball team and captained a basketball squad coached by Indiana legend Tony Hinkle, an innovator who championed the change from brown basketballs to orange ones. Set-shooting five-foot, nine-inch forward Art Cook averaged a team-leading 11 points his junior year, when Butler upset top-ranked Valparaiso's "World's Tallest Team," with its lineup averaging six foot five. Still, he considered himself a baseball player first. Basketball was more popular in Indiana, where the passion for hoops was known as Hoosier Hysteria, but the national pastime suited him better. On the hardwood, his small stature made him literally peripheral—an outside shooter. In baseball, he was the one who took the hill and got a W or L in the box score. "In baseball, the pitcher's in charge. That's the way I liked it," he said. "You're standing there with the ball in your hand. Nothing happens till you put it in play."

It's hard to say how hard he threw. His best fastball might have touched 90 miles an hour. More likely it was 87 or 88. "I'd take a little off," he'd say, "put a little on." Of all the game's truisms, the truest is that hitting is timing, while pitching is upsetting timing, and from an early age Art was adept at that. As a kid, he could spot three pitches: fastball, curve, and changeup. Few teenage pitchers can throw a convincing change, delivering the slowball with the exact motion they use for a fastball. The hitter triggers his fast-twitch swing, but the ball isn't there yet. Strike!

Art attracted the attention of Johnny Riddle, player-manager of the Birmingham Barons. The Barons were a Cincinnati Reds farm club in the Southern Association, a Class A1 team in the parlance of the day, two rungs down from the major leagues. A former backup catcher for four major-league teams, "Mutt" Riddle thought the youngster could help his creaky pitching staff. On February 28, 1944, he signed Arthur Cook to his first pro contract. Art got a $200 signing bonus and $250 a month through the end of the season. Because he was underage, his widowed mother signed her name under his in a shaky hand: *Ella Cook*. Later that week, he left home on a Pennsylvania Railroad train, the South Wind. Like all trains that passed through Southern states in 1943, the South Wind was racially segregated— blacks rode in a section called baggage-coach, and were restricted to two tables behind a curtain in the dining car. The train rolled through Louisville, Bowling Green, and Nashville on its way to Alabama. At Birmingham's turreted Terminal Station, Art Cook lugged his suitcase and duffel bag past a barbershop, a Western Union telegraph booth, and "white" and "colored" bathrooms to the street, where an electrified sign four stories tall welcomed him to BIRMINGHAM, THE MAGIC CITY.

COCKY SMILE OR NONE, he was green as August corn. The average Southern Association player was in his mid-twenties. Eighteen-year-old Art found a room in a Birmingham boardinghouse, but wasn't sure he should eat the meals his landlady prepared, because she was black. Then he got hungry. That was the beginning of his lifelong fondness for butter beans, catfish, and chocolate pie. Bouncing through the South on eye-opening road trips to Atlanta and New Orleans, seeing more of the country than his older siblings or his parents ever had, he learned how much to tip a bellman and which fork to use in a restaurant. He relished the ballplayer's life, the traveling show.

While other young pitchers won with 90-plus-mile-an-hour smoke, Art Cook did it with mirrors. He foiled right-handed batters with a fastball that seemed to rise—a physical impossibility—and a backdoor curve that chipped off the outside corner of the plate. He surprised left-handed hitters with fastballs on their hands. Riddle used Art sparingly that summer: in his first pro season, Cook allowed 15 hits and eight earned runs in 16 innings for an ERA of 4.50. He won his only decision and rode the train home unbeaten, with a professional record of 1–0.

Player-manager Riddle got called up to Cincinnati in 1944. With him gone, the Barons had no use for his teenaged pet project. Art spent most of the next five years pitching for the Kingston (Ontario) Ponies of the Class-C Border League, riding buses back and forth across the Thousand Islands Bridge between Kingston and Watertown, New York, facing the Watertown Athletics, Geneva Robins, Ogdensburg Maples, and Auburn Cayugas, as well as the Ottawa Nationals. Border League fans and players sang two national anthems before games; he came to love "O Canada" almost as much as "The Star-Spangled Banner." Determined to make the majors, he developed a pickoff move that froze runners at first base. A decent hitter and expert bunter, he helped his team at the plate, too, batting .282 one season. In 1948, he batted .268 with three home runs, which made Art Cook the Border League's best-hitting pitcher as well as its best pitcher, period. That was the year he won 21 games, a feat he attributed to "talent and good looks," not to mention a fourth pitch.

He'd had little trouble with amateur hitters on Indiana sandlots, but in the pros, even leadoff men were better hitters than the semipro sluggers he'd faced back home. Middle-of-the-order professionals ignored his edge-of-the-plate stuff and feasted on two-and-one and three-and-one pitches he had to throw over the plate. He needed another weapon.

The screwball's leading early practitioner, New York Giants ace Christy Mathewson, called it a fadeaway because the ball breaks in the opposite direction from the more common curve. The right-handed Mathewson's fadeaway dived away from left-handed batters. Most other hurlers who featured the pitch, from Carl Hubbell to Fernando Valenzuela, have been lefties, using it almost exclusively against right-handed batters. (Renegade righty Mike Marshall, the 1974 Cy Young Award winner, was an exception.) Experimenting with the pitch, Lefty Cook learned to grip the ball across four seams to maximize its spin. At release, he twisted his wrist to the right, imparting the opposite of curveball spin. To picture it, just pretend you're throwing a baseball. A fastball has backspin, like a good jump shot in basketball. To throw a curve, a pitcher twists his thumb upward at release. This gives the ball a sidespin that pitchers call the "natural" spin. It makes the ball move from right to left if you're a right-hander, or from left to right if you're a lefty. But if you release a ball with an unnatural-feeling motion that sends your thumb downward, it spins the opposite way. That's a screwball, one of the toughest pitches to master. Art Cook's was the Border League's best, one of the best in the minors.

Another thing about the screwball: it's hard on the arm. Even pretending to throw one, you may feel a slight twinge in your elbow. Today, due in part to its reputation as an arm-killer, the pitch is almost extinct. No current major leaguer throws it, and some big-league players—including intelligent veteran pitchers—doubt that it's humanly possible to throw such a backward-breaking pitch. They're wrong.

In 1948, mixing his screwball with his curve and sneaky fastball, Art Cook led the Kingston Ponies with a 21–9 record, 27 complete games, and an earned run average of 3.20. No other Ponies pitcher won 10 games. That September, on "Art Cook Appreciation Night" at Kingston's Megaffin Stadium, the Ponies saluted "the Border League's greatest left-hander." He got knocked out of the game in the third inning.

Those were the most vivid days of his life. By then he was twenty-three years old. He and his teammates, many of them farm boys like him, had plenty of time to prowl Border League towns before the 11 o'clock curfew. They played pranks on each other—hotfoots, Heet liniment in the jockstrap, shaving cream or worse in the hat. They barhopped and got into bar fights and, if they were lucky, paired up with young women drawn to their brio and athleticism. Today, ballplayers' groupies get dismissed as "road beef." In the '40s, they were known as Baseball Annies. Some, like Annie Savoy in Ron Shelton's movie *Bull Durham*, tutored rookies in the ways of life and love in the minors. Dad never went into detail about his off-the-field exploits, but one girlfriend thought enough of him to start a scrapbook devoted to Art "Lefty" Cook. I picture her breezing up to the ticket-taker at Megaffin Stadium, home of the Ponies. The ticket-taker knows her, and ushers her in without a ticket. She sits in a sun-splashed field box with players' wives and girlfriends, whistling through her fingers when her man strikes a batter out. She and Art keep each other company on off days and nights, and this is where I stop speculating about his Border League nights, because he's about to meet my mother.

WHEN THE BASEBALL SEASON ENDED, Art returned to Indiana. In 1949, fresh out of Butler, he took a teaching job at Moral Township High School, half an hour from Indianapolis. Moral's red brick schoolhouse sat between U.S. Highway 421 and miles of cornfields. With only seventy students in grades nine through twelve, it was the smallest school in Shelby County. Young Mr. Cook taught English and physical education and coached the baseball and basketball teams. This being Indiana, the basketball team was more important. Out of thirty-three boys enrolled in the school, twenty-two played varsity or junior-varsity basketball.

His hiring made local headlines. "Cook, a southpaw, was well known in Indianapolis," the

Shelbyville News reported. "Art is the property of the Boston Braves and last year led the Border League with a 21–9 record." The first-year coach who summered as a pro ballplayer cut a dashing figure in the hallways at Moral, but his first hoops team was the county's worst, drubbed by taller squads from Morristown High, with its throng of 225 students, and mighty Shelbyville, which had more than 1,000. (Big-town Shelbyville, population 11,000, drew crowds of 2,000 to home games, where fans mocked rural Moral by waving toy tractors.) Coach Cook's Moral Hawks went 4–17 in 1949–50. The next season, he handed his players a mimeographed page listing his standards for athletes. "I'd rather have a B student with an A attitude than a A student with an B attitude," it began, listing team rules:

No drinking, no smoking, no misuse of drugs.

Maintain a proper diet. Avoid sweets.

Keep your male-female relationship in proper perspective.

Maintain a high standard of: personal appearance, dress, hair-cuts, language—do not be loud and boisterous; avoid profanity; think and speak positively.

Respect authority—coaches, teachers, officials, parents.

Be composed and determined in defeat, and humble and gracious in success.

He also drilled his undersized boys in Tony Hinkle's offense with its multiple passes, picks, and screens. He'd blow his whistle to bark at a kid who was out of position, then blow it a minute later to praise the same kid. "We loved him. I'm not BS-ing you," one of his players, Dave Powell, told me years later. "Nobody was ever more fair than him. And he was a better athlete than we were, so we listened to him. And then we started winning."

Moral Township won its first county tournament in Coach Cook's second season. Next came what the *News* called "a six-year streak of near-dominance." His Hawks went 22–2 and 21–2, with 34 straight victories, a county record that still stands. In a story headed DAVID-GOLIATH TALE UNFOLDING AT MORAL, Jimmie Angelopoulos of the *Indianapolis Times* asked readers, "What's Cooking? Why, Art Cook. He's the quiet, funda-mentally sound former Butler baseball and basketball disciple. Cook is coaching Moral. And now Moral is cooking with gas." Tiny Moral was on its way to a second, third, and fourth Shelby County title. The Hawks once scored 105 points in a game at a time when winning teams often scored 50. They beat Knightstown in the gym that served as Hickory High's home court in the movie *Hoosiers*. Art got so many handshakes and backslaps in the halls at Moral that he was sometimes late to class. Along the way, another newcomer caught his eye.

The other young English teacher on the faculty was a big-city girl. An Indianapolis stockbroker's daughter, educated in the city's best Catholic schools, Patricia Parker had been to London and Paris. With her proper diction and spruce skirts and blouses, Miss Parker seemed a little out of place in the cornfields of Shelby County, but like almost every unmarried woman in the township, she had noticed the young coach with a whistle around his neck. She couldn't help being a little dazzled by his looks, his confidence, his manners. When he asked her out to dinner, she said yes. More sophisticated than most men from rural Indiana, he held doors and chairs for her and put a protective hand on the small of her back as they moved through a crowd. Soon they were an item. Schoolgirls giggled when Mr. Cook passed her classroom, while his players needled him about keeping his male-female relationship in perspective. Miss Parker's Catholic, socially ambitious parents thought Art Cook was a little uncouth, not to mention Baptist, but they enjoyed reading about him in the papers, and in time he won them over. In 1954, Art Cook and Patricia Parker married in a Catholic ceremony at Our Lady of Lourdes church in Indianapolis.

The newlyweds honeymooned in Chicago. Toasting their future together in the Allerton Hotel's penthouse bar, the Tip Top Tap, Art asked his bride what they should do on their first full day as husband and wife. "Let's see a play," she said.

The next afternoon, they saw Zero Mostel in Rodgers and Hammerstein's *Me and Juliet*. "The next day, we went to a ballgame," she recalled, "and the day after that, and the day after that. I spent most of my honeymoon at Wrigley Field and Comiskey Park and enjoyed every inning. Then we drove to Ontario, where he played ball that summer."

At twenty-eight, with more than 1,200 professional innings under his belt, he had thrown at least a thousand screwballs along with countless fastballs and curves, earning a reputation as a pitcher who took the ball whenever his team needed him. Five years after setting the Butler University record for most innings pitched, he tossed those 27 complete games for Kingston. Three years later, he pulled off the "Iron Man" stunt for the Kitty League's Union City (Tennessee) Greyhounds, pitching and winning both ends of a doubleheader. He shut out the Madisonville (Tennessee) Miners 1–0 in the first game and beat them 3–2 in the nightcap, stealing third and scoring the winning run on a sacrifice fly.

Two weeks later, he repeated the feat, topping the Mayfield (Kentucky) Clothiers in both ends of a doubleheader. In a story headed COOK "IRON MAN" OVER MAYFIELD, the Union City *Daily Messenger* described "tough, gruelling innings" in which Lefty Cook, "a tough, clutch pitcher, jumped into the Kitty League record books" by scattering twelve hits and nine walks in four hours of baseball. Nobody was counting pitches, but he must have thrown two hundred that night.

Back in Indianapolis, sportswriter Val Dickman celebrated an unofficial professional baseball record: two Iron Man stunts in fifteen days. "A new Cook is burning up the Kitty League with a menu of fastballs," he wrote, "and with accompanying fanfare has changed the Tennessee Waltz of the Union City Greyhounds into a Hoosier fox trot. The chef is Art Cook, former Butler University baseball and basketball star. He's been serving sizzlers across the plates of Kitty League batters in doubleheaders."

That was the year Art released a pitch and felt something snap inside his arm.

2

The Talker
★ *and the Thinker* ★

RON AND IKE DAVIS

Nuts! It's just crazy-butt nuts."

Ron Davis was throwing and talking, two things he's good at. Throwing to teenage hitters, talking about baseball's injury epidemic. Davis, 59, coaches the Sidewinders, an elite travel team of middle schoolers in Scottsdale, Arizona. Each of the thirteen-year-old Sidewinders pays $200 a month to be part of Team Davis Baseball. The program fields teams in three age groups, from the twelve-year-olds he calls his "midgets" to fifteen-year-olds with incipient mustaches. All his teams are called the Sidewinders, and they usually wind up thumping their youth-league competition. On the day I met Davis, a 1981 All-Star reliever for the New York Yankees, his thirteen-year-olds had a record of seven wins and no losses.

Toeing the rubber on a chalky, sun-bleached mound, he fed them batting-practice straightballs. "Obliques," he said, picking a ball from a white plastic bucket. "Intercostals. Tommy John surgery." To Davis, baseball's injury plague is a scandal. He told me he figured he had thrown an average of about two hundred pitches a day since he was a kid. That adds up to about 3,650,000 pitches. And he never had a sore arm.

He spat a gob of tobacco. "Did you know there's been four thousand Tommy John surgeries in the last twenty years? Do you know how many there were in my day? One. Tommy John!"

Davis and John were teammates for three years. In 1979 a post-surgery Tommy John won 21 games for the Yankees while Davis won 14 coming out of the bullpen. Those were the Bronx Zoo–era Yankees of Billy Martin, Reggie Jackson, Catfish Hunter, Ron Guidry, Goose Gossage, Luis Tiant, and Thurman Munson, a raucous bunch whose nights on the town grew as gnarly as their facial hair. Martin, the manager, had the world's shortest fuse. He was always ready to go after a barfly who criticized a Yankee. Or to go after a Yankee himself. Often as not, the players held Billy back to prevent a midnight free-for-all. When they failed, it made headlines.

"We lost Thurman that year; he died flying his plane," Davis recalled. "That was such a blow to us. And Reggie? Well, he was never part of our crew. Reggie didn't have a friend on the team. But the rest of us, man, we were brothers." Going into the '79 season, the Yanks revamped their bullpen, shipping All-Star reliever Sparky Lyle to Texas. Lyle was a mustachioed leader of the clubhouse frat, known for dropping trou and plopping his naked butt on top of teammates' birthday cakes. But Gossage threw harder. With Lyle gone, Gossage took over the ninth inning. When he came in, the game was as good as won. Before the Gossage era, relief pitchers were almost always failed starters, the dregs of a team's pitching staff, but once other clubs saw how Billy Martin used Gossage, they began looking to their own pitching staffs for a new sort of ace, a late-inning specialist. A closer.

While Gossage pitched the ninth inning and sometimes the eighth, Ron Davis handled the seventh and sometimes the eighth. Gossage's fastball touched 100 miles an hour. Davis threw almost as hard. Together they were the most intimidating relief duo the game had ever seen.

A gangly, talkative Texan with a curly mop of auburn hair, Davis was so nearsighted that he needed glasses to see the catcher's signals. His wire-rimmed specs gave him a perpetually squinty expression that suited his view of the world. "I was surprised to be in the middle of all that Yankee stuff," he said. "Amazed, really. Just seeing my name in a box score made me think, 'Well, heck, I must be in the big leagues!'" The first All-Star to pitch almost exclusively in the seventh and eighth innings, he was the first to be known for that in-between role. Ron Davis was the first famous setup man.

In 1981, he fanned eight California Angels in a row, setting a league record. He pitched in an All-Star Game and a World Series. "I had my moments," he allowed. "Those were the days of wine, women, and song. Now I'm down to mostly song."

Davis's cackle was a note or two higher than you'd expect for a man his size. Six foot four and 200 pounds in his playing days, he was rounder now, closer to 250, comfortably filling an extra-large Under Armour golf shirt. Still, he was quick on his feet. He carried his weight the way my dad did, with the grace of a lighter man.

I asked which of his Sidewinders might be a major-league prospect. "There's no telling," he said. In twenty-five years of coaching youth baseball, he had yet to spot a surefire prospect. "Not even Bryce Harper," he said. At thirteen, ripping pitches all over the lot for Team Davis Baseball, the future Washington Nationals star "looked good, not great. He hadn't grown into his body. That's the thing about thirteen. Your talent's got to grow, but so do you." Harper grew. At six feet, three inches, he would be a foot taller and almost a hundred pounds heavier as a Nationals rookie in 2012 than he was as a 2005 Sidewinder. "Size is so big in this game, and you can't predict it," Davis said. Fans meeting big leaguers for the first time are often surprised by their size. A study of major-league players from 1960 to 2010 found that pitchers were the tallest, averaging just over six foot two. First basemen were next, at six foot one and a half, while second basemen and shortstops were the runts of the roster at five foot eleven. And players get bigger all the time. "Some of these boys have skills, but they're still making lines on the wall and checking their height every night. One thing you won't see in the big leagues is a five-foot-eight first baseman."

Even the smallest Sidewinder came equipped with big-time gear. Shortstop Austin Vance swung a glistening Mako BBCOR aluminum-graphite composite bat, ivory in color with orange trim. More lively than wood or ordinary aluminum, the Mako was a tube of woven graphite with an aluminum skin, for what ads call "unmatched bat speed and a massive sweet spot." It cost $399. Jeff Vance, Austin's dad, said his son's glove set him back $350. "Three-fitty for a ball glove!" Davis marveled. Yet he understood why his players wanted such equipment. Top-quality leather is tackier and lasts longer, saving fielders the chore of breaking in a new glove every year or two. And while an old-fashioned $100 aluminum bat might launch a fly ball 200 feet, the same pitch hit the same way with Austin's Mako would go 250 or 260. That's the difference between a fly ball and a homer. Hard-hit grounders off a Mako bat zipped through the infield faster, too, turning groundouts into base hits.

Many suburban families can afford to spend $700 and up for a bat and a glove or mitt (once and for all: catchers and first basemen wear mitts, everybody else wears a glove), plus hundreds or thousands more for spikes, batting gloves, food supplements, personal trainers, sports psychologists, and other perks. When his teams entered out-of-state tournaments, Davis would load several kids into his Chevy Tahoe and drive them to California or Colorado, but most of the players would fly. The same wasn't true for the mostly-minority teams from South Phoenix that the Sidewinders routinely trounced in local games. "That's got to do with Jimmy Rollins's question," Davis said. Rollins, the veteran big-league shortstop, has wondered why there are fewer African-American major leaguers than there used to be. Some pundits say the pace of baseball is too slow to hold inner-city kids' attention, or that there aren't enough baseball diamonds in black neighborhoods, or that it takes too long to make the majors—four or five years for all but the most precocious, while football players go directly from college to the NFL, and basketball phenoms sometimes jump straight from high school to the pros. ESPN's Stephen A. Smith claimed that young black athletes "don't trust baseball." In his view, they suspect the minor leagues are stacked with chaw-chewing white coaches who favor white players, "while in basketball, if you're good enough, you're going to the NBA." But in this case, Occam's razor may actually be a $399 aluminum bat. According to Davis, minority kids from South Phoenix and elsewhere are beaten before they step into the batter's box, simply because of their equipment. Their long balls get caught while the Sidewinders' shots clear the wall. "It's not every hit or even every game," he told me, "but in the long run a kid with a crummy old bat hasn't got as much of a chance, and baseball's all about the long run. Baseball wears you down. So if you're a kid with some talent, are you gonna hang in there for seven or eight years and *maybe* be one of the one in a million who make it? Or go pick up a basketball?"

His travel teamers, almost all of them white, have won eight state championships and two national titles. But while they cheer and fist-bump each other and sometimes go for pizza after victories, they're more a collection of free agents than the neighborhood-based teams Davis and I grew up playing for. Their parents pay Davis to hone the kids' talents, not win team trophies. Job one is to make the local high school team. "There's a load of talent in this part of the country," one dad told me on the sidelines at Cholla Park. His son would attend a high school that had three thousand students. "That's fifteen hundred boys."

Making the varsity baseball team would be a tall order.

Davis feels the weight of his players' ambitions. He spends about fifteen hours a week running practices and games, and fifteen more fielding calls and texts from players and their parents. Riley Barrett, a straight-A+ student, was offered a chance to test out of high school and go straight to college. He said no. What was he going to do, make a college team at the age of fourteen? Riley chose to endure four boring years of high school physics and pre-calculus classes to keep his baseball hopes alive.

One of his teammates had other worries. Jesse—not his real name—gloved a grounder behind second base, then cast a glance toward the parking lot. "Looking for his mom's car," another player said. "Hoping he won't see it." Jesse's parents were divorcing. His mother wouldn't let him play baseball, so he played only on the days he spent with his father and counted on his friends to keep their mouths shut. How long did he think he could he keep his secret? "I dunno," he told me. "I just want to max out." To get as good as he could. To give his talent a chance, just in case it was big-league talent.

"I love that boy," Davis said when Jesse was out of earshot. "He's got a hard road. Some of these others, I don't want to say *spoiled* . . ." So he didn't say "spoiled." He said his thirteen-year-old suburbanites lived in "a self-esteem world." They grew up hearing their parents cheer their every move. "They cheer *strikeouts*. It's like, 'Nice screwup, Johnny. You struck out so well!' " He had seen good players quit the game after their first slumps in high school or college ball. Unprepared for adversity, "they give up. They can't dig deep because there's nowhere to dig." Davis wouldn't mind toughening his players up a little, but there are limits. He could make them run laps for missing signals and other miscues, but only a couple of laps. If one of them were to faint or throw up, Coach Ron might get sued.

Still, they see him as a taskmaster. "He yells at us," a Sidewinder told me in the dugout. Another said, "Yeah, Ron's a hard-ass. The kind of coach you either love or hate."

Davis had been listening. He waved them toward third base, pretending to crack a whip.

They finished practice with a round of "gold glove," a fielding drill. The boys lined up at third. Davis smacked sharp grounders. Field the ball and make a strong throw to first and you stay in the game; fail and you're out. With each round, the survivors moved over to shortstop, then second base, and so on.

"Baseball is *what?*" Davis barked, slapping a grounder.

"A thinking man's game!" the boys called back.

After practice, they scattered into a parking lot

dotted with luxury cars and SUVs. Nobody stuck around to play a pickup game. Like suburban athletes all over the country, they led tightly scheduled lives. They played sports to get an edge on other kids their age, for advancement of one kind or another, and only incidentally for fun.

"Ron, I can't make it Saturday. Got soccer," one boy yelled.

"Soccer? That's a communist game."

"I've got to go to church Sunday," another said.

"And miss the Church of Ron?"

Soon the parking lot was empty except for Davis's SUV. He spent ten minutes wandering the long grass beyond the outfield, kicking weeds, picking up balls and dropping them in his bucket. He hated to leave any behind. Every week or so, he would drive to Salt River Fields, the Arizona Diamondbacks and Colorado Rockies' spring-training complex, to replenish his supply. While March is prime time for ball hunters, the teams hold extended spring training all summer for players rehabbing injuries. "The groundskeepers pick up the balls that stay on the fields, but not the homers," he said. The desert kept the homers until Davis came for them. A minor-league ball is worth about eight dollars and a major-league ball retails for about eighteen.

Davis handed me a ball. "That's a big-league baseball," he said. Its seams were tighter than those of the minor-league variety, making the ball feel smoother. That's worse for pitchers, because lower seams meet less air resistance. As a result, breaking pitches break a fraction less. Sinkers and cutters go a little straighter. Tight seams also make a ball slightly harder. A pitch that breaks less because its seams are lower may rocket back at the pitcher at 120 miles an hour. Davis remembers a liner that nearly rearranged his face. "I threw my hand up and the ball broke my finger," he said. "People asked why I did that, since the finger was better-looking than the face."

A child of the 1960s and '70s, he played in a more flake-friendly era. "We were characters, not robots. We were starting to make some real money, but not millions and millions." When the players went on strike in 1981, he took a job as a waiter in an Upper East Side restaurant. He liked that gig so much that he did a stint waiting tables at the Hyatt Regency in Kansas City, where two walkways collapsed that summer, killing 113. Davis was one of the first on the scene. He pulled survivors from the rubble. Hailed as a hero, he said, "Aw, there was lots of us running to help. I was the only ballplayer, that's all." Then he got rocked in the '81 World Series. The Yankees shipped him to Minnesota, where he saved 108 games, still fourth on the Twins' all-time list, while developing a rep as a late-inning goat. His team-record 14 blown saves in 1984 unfolded in such bombs-bursting-in-the-upper-deck fashion that Twins fans dubbed him "Boom-Boom" Davis.

"It's an easy game when you're going good," he said, "and just about impossible when you're not. I'm still learning that, seeing it happen to my son."

RON DAVIS WAS THIRTY-ONE, creaky for a ball-player of his generation, when his second son was born in Minnesota. Ron and his wife, Millie, whom he'd met while boarding with her family as a penny-pinching minor leaguer, named the boy Isaac Benjamin after Millie's two grandfathers, in keeping with Jewish tradition. Millie was Jewish while Ron was "Baptist, pretty much, but not the Baseball Chapel type." Later that year, the Twins traded him to the Chicago Cubs, who released him. He signed with the San Francisco Giants, who sold his contract to the Yakult Swallows of Japan's Central League. That's why one of Ike Davis's earliest memories is of fireworks over Tokyo's Meiji Jingu Stadium. Ron's Japanese teammates dubbed the tyke "Little McEnroe" for his frizzy reddish hair and fizzy energy.

Ron retired in 1988. The Davises settled in Scottsdale. They liked the dry heat. Their first son, Ellison, preferred football, but Ike was a baseball kid from the get-go. He began hitting fungoes when he was still in diapers. He'd grab a roll of Reynolds Wrap from his mother, crumple a strip of the foil, toss the lump of foil, and smack it with the rest of the roll, saying, "Ball, ball!" Ron went on to coach his youth-league teams, and for once there were no gripes from other parents about which kid batted fourth. From the age of five, like almost every future major leaguer, Ike dominated. He was better than all the other kids his age, better than local all-stars two and three years older than he was. He walloped homers, pitched no-hitters, ranged from deep short into dugouts to catch pop-ups. Ike grew out of his rubber-cleated Little League shoes into size 11 steel spikes and starred in baseball, football, and soccer at Scottsdale's Chaparral High School. In baseball, he led the Chaparral Firebirds to three state championships, batting .447 with a pitching record of 23 wins, no losses, and 14 saves.

"He was pretty doggone better than fair," Ron said. Like a lot of dads, he thought his kid was special. "I wanted to think he had big-league talent, but like I said, you never know. Every kid who thinks he's going to make it comes from a place where he's head and shoulders over all the others, and everybody *knows* he's going to be famous. But you know what? There's a lot of places out there. Most of those boys wind up coaching or selling cars. I know some who work at Walmart. And I let Isaac know that. One thing he had was the benefit of my experience. He always knew how far it was from high school to the big leagues."

Ike was a senior at Chaparral High when he played in a pair of national high school showcases in Baltimore and Albuquerque. He won the first game, pitching a 1–0 shutout. "The other game he hits a three-run tater and pitches the last two innings for the save," Ron recalled. They named him MVP in both games.

Despite his high school numbers, Ike was ignored in Major League Baseball's 2004 draft of amateur players. General managers knew he was headed to Arizona State, his hero Barry Bonds's school. In his first game for the nationally ranked Sun Devils, Ike pitched, batted third, and homered. That was the day Ron thought, "He's going to be a major leaguer."

"Not that I told him that. Let him find out for himself."

Ike batted .352 for Arizona State while firing 94 mph fastballs. He mixed in a cutter and a wicked changeup, a pitch few teenage hurlers can master. "My dad taught me that one," he said. Ike grew to six foot four with broad lumberjack shoulders. The Tampa Bay Rays selected him in the 19th round of the 2005 amateur draft. The Davises knew that nineteenth-rounders earn peanuts in the minors, watching early-round bonus babies get fast-tracked to the big leagues. "Don't sign," Ron told his son. "Not yet." Ike returned to ASU, where he batted .385 his junior year with 16 homers and 76 RBIs in a 52-game season. His patience paid off when the Mets made him their first-round selection in the 2008 draft—eighteenth overall, behind Buster Posey and Pedro Álvarez but ahead of Craig Kimbrel, Dee Gordon, and Lance Lynn.

"My dad told me New York's got the best fans," Ike said. "Every game's do-or-die. He said he loved New York and I would, too."

Ike signed for $1,575,000. Father and son celebrated with a sip of Ron's favorite single malt, then turned to Ike's next decision. Was he a pitcher or a hitter? Not even Babe Ruth could do both at the game's highest level. The Mets left the choice to the Davises.

They were similar in size, but not in temperament. Both dipped tobacco. Ron enjoyed a dram of Lagavulin, while Ike was more of a beer man. Ron was the talker with the goofy sense of humor, while Ike was more stoic, a man of fewer words.

"I like playing every day," he said.

"Well, that's a starting point," Ron said.

They kicked it around for a few days. "How many guys throw as hard as you do?" Ron asked. He wasn't pushing pitching, just playing devil's agent. "Suppose you pitch. You're a left-hander throwing 95. There's not many of those. You might get to the big leagues faster—a couple years instead of three or four."

"Two years," Ike said. "That'd be 2010."

He conferred with his agent, Lou Jon Nero of Octagon Sports. Nero helped Ike avoid such pitfalls as signing an equipment deal right away. "That's a trap," Ike recalled. Many minor leaguers, dazzled by the thought of representing Nike or Under Armour, sign multiyear contracts for free cleats or shirts plus $500 a year. "Then you get to the majors, you're an up-and-coming rookie worth twenty thousand a year, and you're stuck at five hundred."

Spurning lowball endorsements was an easier call than deciding which position Ike would play. Ron's role was to help his son make the first key decision of his pro career. As he saw it, "My job as a parent was to talk about the options, including which option would keep the others open." In that way, he was like any concerned dad. "If he'd been a different kind of kid, the valedictorian who didn't play sports, we might have been talking about law school or medical school. I didn't want to push him one way or the other. I wanted to be his adviser. He knew I'd been there myself, and he knew I was on his side. Not every kid has that."

A casino choice, Ron called it. Which decision would optimize the odds, not only of Ike's reaching the majors, but of getting there soon? Timing mattered because an early arrival starts a player's service-time clock sooner. In today's game, service time ranks second only to stats in determining a man's value. Under the collective bargaining agreement between management and the players' association, some players with two-plus years in the majors have an advantage worth millions of dollars. Those with the most time in the major leagues—the top 22 percent in each year's class of players who have two to three years' time in the majors—qualify for arbitration. They are the so-called "super-twos" who stand to get rich. It's an edge that can come down to months or even days. That's why teams keep surefire prospects in the minors until June every year—to prevent them from playing enough games to earn super-two status two years down the road. It happened to Stephen Strasburg and Giancarlo Stanton in 2010, Wil Myers in 2013, and Gregory Polanco in 2014. Like NBA also-rans tanking late-season games to get a better shot at a lottery pick, major league teams often keep their phenoms down on the farm until June or July, choosing to field an inferior product for a few weeks or months in order to save millions in the long run.

If Ike was as good as his dad thought he was, he might be pitching for the Mets by 2010. That could mean super-two status and an extra $5 million (or more) two to three years later. Five million was about twice what Ron earned in his eleven-year big-league career. "Pitching could get you there faster," Ron said. "But if you pitch, it's harder to go back to the other option. You get slotted. Pitchers have a hell of a time coming back as hitters."

Ike said, "That makes no sense."

"It's how they think. If you fail as a pitcher, you're a loser. But if you come up as a hitter and it doesn't work out, and then you show 'em a 90-plus fastball, they'll say, 'What a discovery!' " The decision boiled down to Ron's longer view—hit first, and optimize your options—versus Ike's drive to reach the majors as fast as he could.

"You're a grown man, Isaac," Ron said. "You've got last call."

Ike nodded. "I know."

FIRST BASEMAN IKE DAVIS reached the top of the Mets' farm system in two years. He starred in the low minors for the Brooklyn Cyclones in 2008 and smacked 20 homers for two higher-level teams in 2009. Along the way, he developed a trademark play. Chasing a pop-up into foul territory, he would clasp the dugout railing with his bare hand, lean over the railing, and catch the ball while tumbling into the dugout. Ron winced the first time he saw it. Why risk your neck to get a minor-league out? But fans, coaches, and teammates, especially pitchers, loved Ike for it. His dugout dives inspired the first Ike Davis souvenir: a bobblehead-style figure in a Cyclones uniform, upside-down behind a waist-high railing.

He phoned his dad almost every day until Ron

learned to text. Ron's plus-size thumbs sent mostly typos—*Nicce gmong!!!*—till he got the hang of texting. Ike began the 2010 season with the Triple-A Buffalo Bisons while veteran Mike Jacobs played first for the parent club. Ron followed the Bisons online at MiLB.com, the Minor League Baseball website, and listened to their WWKB-AM gamecasts on satellite radio. He also kept tabs on the Mets, who were getting little production from Jacobs. Ike was batting .364 on April 19 and was penciled in at cleanup that night, when Bisons manager Ken Oberkfell pulled him aside. "No BP for you," Oberkfell said. "They sent a car." Ike was to get dressed, get in the car, and go to the Buffalo airport. No handshakes, no goodbyes.

Ike hurried to the clubhouse. Grabbing his gym bag and shaving kit, he hustled to the black car outside Buffalo's Coca-Cola Field. The first call he made was to Scottsdale. "I just got called up, Daddy," he said. "I'm going to New York."

3

★ *Miracles* ★

DAN HAREN SR. AND DAN HAREN JR.

A rubber-coated ball hopped through a rubber-coated in-field. The batter took off for first base. She rounded first at top speed, sun glinting off the spokes of her wheelchair. A minute later, Hillary crossed the plate with an inside-the-park home run.

Laughing, she said that was the best part of baseball. Not hitting homers. "Running the bases."

Hillary doesn't run bases the way most ball-players do. She has never walked. Still, like thousands of other disabled young people around the world, she's a Miracle League star.

"EACH MIRACLE LEAGUE IS SPECIAL in its own way. Like the kids," says Dan Haren. He runs Dan Haren Stadium in Scottsdale, Arizona, a wheelchair-accessible $2.3 million ball field next door to the Cholla Park diamond where Ron Davis coaches his elite Sidewinders, the kids with the $400 bats. Dan Haren Stadium is named not for

Dan but for his son, Dan Haren Jr., the $10 million-a-year major-league pitcher who helped pay for it.

"It's a payback thing," says Dan Sr., a bright-eyed, silver-haired man who favors Hawaiian shirts. "I was a pretty good athlete—played against Roger Staubach in college, and then baseball in the Navy—but never made the pros. Later on, I introduced my son Danny to baseball, and he was a prodigy. And from Little League in Southern California through high school until he graduated from Pepperdine, do you know how many of his games I missed? Five."

During their youth baseball years, the Harens couldn't help noticing less-lucky families. "We'd hop out of the car and see parents spend five or ten minutes unloading their disabled child from a van, a child who could only watch the game." Dan Sr. felt for those kids and their families but seldom stopped to talk with them. He was busy with baseball-dad duties: wearing out his knees catching his talented son after school, driving Danny to workouts and tournaments, video-taping his games for study on the VCR, and interceding with the occasional numbskull youth-league coach who wanted to overuse the boy or change his motion.

Like many baseball dads, Dan Sr. acted as both father and coach. His duty, as he saw it, was to protect his son from whatever might impede his progress toward the big leagues—against Danny's wishes, if necessary. "Kids want to do kid things," he says. "Sometimes you have to keep the goal in mind for them." He pushed Danny hard, forbidding him to play with friends until the boy threw to his dad for half an hour after school.

"I hated him for it," Dan Jr. recalled decades later. "He pushed me, and I hated it, but it made me better."

In 2001, the St. Louis Cardinals chose Pepperdine All-American Dan Haren Jr. in the second round of the major league draft. After a trade to Oakland, he became a mainstay of the A's rotation. He started the 2007 All-Star Game for the American League, and went on to win 15 games with a 3.07 ERA that year. At twenty-six, Danny Haren was everything his dad hoped he would be—a star, a multimillionaire, a consummate pro—even if he wasn't quite cut out for the big-league lifestyle. But more on that later.

After the 2007 season, the A's traded their best pitcher to the Arizona Diamondbacks for prospects, including eighteen-year-old Carlos González. In Phoenix, the tall, scruffily bearded right-hander became one of the National League's top starters, going 16–8 and then 14–10, slicing corners off the plate with a panoply of cutters, splitters, curves, changeups, and sneaky fastballs, all delivered from a motion that had an odd, stop-motion hesitation in the middle. He was a thinker on the mound, reacting to a batter's reaction to the previous pitch. In his second year with the Diamondbacks, Haren struck out 223 while walking only 38, quite a feat for a hurler whose fastball topped out at 89.

In 2008 he signed a four-year, $44.75 million contract with the Diamondbacks. That was the year his wife, Jessica, gave birth to a boy named Rhett. "Danny asked me and his mom to move to Arizona to help with the baby," Dan Sr. recalls. "I said, 'Um, let me talk to your mom,' but she was halfway to the airport before I hung up the phone."

While his wife did diaper duty in Scottsdale, Dan Sr. felt a little lost. He thought back to the sight of disabled children being trundled out of vans at youth-league games, kids who could only dream of playing ball like Danny did. "Those kids loved baseball too, and their families had the same dreams we did," he says. "Not to send a son to the major leagues, maybe, but sharing the game. I mean, what's better than cheering your child as he comes around third base? I think kids need to hear that, even if they're in a wheelchair. So I turned to Danny." With contributions from Dan Jr., the Diamondbacks, and Arizona charities, Dan Sr. built an all-access showplace in Scottsdale, in the same city park where Ron Davis's Sidewinders practice on a grass-and-dirt field. Dan Haren Stadium, one of the most elaborate Miracle League fields on earth, features wheelchair-accessible dugouts and batting cages, lights for night games, a two-story scoreboard, and a just-for-fun swing set that lifts wheelchairs into the air. While big leaguer Dan Jr. flew around the country all summer, pitching for $425,000 per start, his dad stayed in Scottsdale, scheduling Miracle League games for hundreds of players, pairing up players with volunteer buddies, acting as the league's executive director, chief cheerleader, and stadium announcer.

"It's going, going . . . off the wall!" he shouted one Sunday as a wheelchair-bound batter sent a bouncer to the outfield fence.

"People ask me, 'What's the Miracle League? A sport or a charity?' " he said. "I say we want to be a life-changer. One of our moms, she has an autistic boy who's had a really hard time, but he had a good day on our field. She told me we gave her son the first smile he ever had."

Miracle League Baseball began in 2000, when civic leaders in Conyers, Georgia, built a baseball diamond for special-needs children. The idea was inspired by a wheelchair-bound youngster who showed up every week to cheer his brother's Little League team. Seven-year-old Mike Moore became the town's superfan, but he dreamed of fair territory. "I want to play," he said. With help from local businesses and charities, Mike and twenty other disabled kids began playing a game they called wheelchair baseball.

The rules were new. In what became known as Miracle League ball, nobody strikes out, grounds out, flies out, or gets tagged out. In this game, the rule is three strikes and you're up. Everyone is safe on every play. Each player bats once per inning. The field, too, is safe, cushioned with a layer of foam rubber. Each player has a volunteer "buddy" to help swing the bat, field and throw the ball, and high-five or fist-bump his or her player when they score a run together. At first, the league's motto, "Every child deserves a chance to play baseball," applied to a couple dozen disabled kids in Georgia. Within a year, there were 150 players, then 1,000. By 2014 there were 315 Miracle Leagues in the U.S., Canada, Australia, and Mexico, making Miracle League Baseball an international pastime that reached more than 200,000 players and their families.

I took in a Miracle League game in New York on Father's Day 2014. Star-spangled bunting hung from the padded center-field fence 125 feet from home plate. "We're trying to make the game accessible to kids of wildly different abilities," said Steve Madey, the sixty-seven-year-old director of the Westchester County league. "The question is, how do you mix children in wheelchairs with blind kids and children with autism? Autistic kids may lack attention span, but some of 'em can run and throw and hit. We've had a few knock it over the fence. It's hard to put them in the same game with cerebral-palsy kids using chairs and walkers." So Madey invented Spectrumball, a program designed for autistic players.

Gangly Ryan Maldonado, fifteen years old, sported baseball pants with stirrup socks. Ryan had been dressed and ready to go since daybreak, but now he had to wait out a typical distraction. When a ball bounced off a player's foot, the autistic child screeched until his buddy calmed him down. Madey cried, "Play ball." Ryan smacked a humpbacked liner over second base. As it rolled to the center-field fence, he ran to the bleachers and gave his dad a Father's Day hug.

Then there was Chase Sadowski, taking a walk. Seven-year-old Chase had steel braces on his legs. Cerebral palsy had kept him in a wheelchair until his father, Walter, discovered the Upsee, a harness that allows Chase to stand upright while strapped to Walter's legs. The boy's feet go into special sandals mounted between his dad's shoes, leaving Chase's hands free to hold a bat. Thanks to the Miracle League and the Upsee, Walter said, "Chase gets to be a baseball fan and something he likes even better—an athlete. A ballplayer."

Father and son took the field with stiff-legged steps, moving in tandem as if the boy were piloting a giant robot. "Daddy, c'mon, c'mon," Chase said. "I'm up!"

IN 2010, Scottsdale's leading Miracle League sponsor left town. Dan Haren—the younger, scruffy one—joined the Los Angeles Angels of Anaheim. He moved back to Southern California with his wife and two toddlers. His parents stayed in Arizona. Dan Sr. wasn't ready to leave the Scottsdale Miracle League behind. Now he followed Danny on TV, online, and in their near-nightly phone calls. He learned not to call his son too soon after a loss, and there were more losses now. In 2011, the year he turned thirty, Haren went 16–10 for the Angels. A year later, he went 12–13. "Danny did fine in Anaheim. He won 33 games in two and a half years," his father says. "But he took the losses hard. Sometimes he got down on himself."

Haren still made a fan of Angels manager Mike Scioscia, who lauded his command of his pitches. "He throws very few clams," Scioscia said. "Look around the game and you won't find anybody who competes better than Dan Haren." Which didn't keep the Angels from letting him go. Haren then signed with the Washington Nationals and spent the 2013 season playing home games three thousand miles from his family. Lonely and miserable, he went 10–14 for the Nationals. Then, in the winter of 2013–14, he signed a one-year, $10 million contract with the Dodgers. Ten million dollars was a mild disappointment. It was a pay cut—the first of his career—of $3 million. Other arms with fewer good seasons were selling for millions more, but Haren was thirty-two, with a fastball that now leaned closer to 85 than 90.

"He was still a good, good pitcher, All-Star caliber," says Dan Sr., who has mellowed from high-pressure dad to become his son's biggest fan. Twenty years after their mandatory after-school throwing sessions, the pressure on Danny came from Danny himself. Nearing his mid-thirties, still new to failure on the field, he couldn't help wondering who he was, if not a baseball star.

Sports bloggers were less than enthused with the Dodgers' new starter, who joined a rotation headed by the near-unhittable Clayton Kershaw. Compared to Kershaw, Haren was an innings eater, maybe no more than a "replacement-level" starting pitcher, not much better than a minimum-wage rookie making $500,000. He accepted the Dodgers' offer for two reasons. He wanted to stay in Southern California with his wife and kids, and he wanted to prove himself again. He had already pitched more than 2,000 innings and won 129 major-league games, but over the past two seasons he had won 22 and lost 27 with an ERA of 4.86. Was he finished?

The Dodgers offered an incentive: a clause that would give him a player option worth another $10 million if he pitched 180 innings in 2014. "I liked that," he says. "Pure performance. Yes or no."

The option was a gamble for both sides. The Dodgers, hedging their risk, were basically betting that Haren would get hurt. He was taking the other side of the wager, betting $10 million that he would be more durable in his twelfth big-league season than he'd been in his tenth and eleventh. "I was thirty-three years old," he says. "I was coming off a couple bad years. What was I supposed to do, give up?"

WATCHING HAREN PITCH, the first thing you notice is that hiccup in the middle of his delivery. If you meet him on or off the field, you might spot the names inscribed on his arm—Rhett and Ella, his kids' names. His son, Rhett, turned six during the 2014 season. Ella was four. Right-hander Haren got the tattoos on his left forearm so that their names press close to his heart when he pulls his glove to his chest during his windup.

He's hardly the only doting dad in the big leagues, but you'd have a hard time finding one who works harder at the role. Ballplayers who have children seldom talk about how hard it can be to stay involved in their kids' lives from March through September. Kids crave routine, and a ballplayer's schedule gives them anything but. Even when Dad's home, he's gone till midnight or later. When he's on the road, time zones make things worse. And you can forget weekends—he'll be at the park all day.

Dan Haren had been a workhorse ever since he reconciled himself to his father's pushy parenting. From 2005 through 2014, a full decade of major-league play, no pitcher threw more innings than Haren's 2,113⅔. But by the time I caught up with him in August 2014, he was scuffling. His mediocre season got worse on a bright Sunday at Dodger Stadium, where the Milwaukee Brewers knocked him off the mound early. A CBS Sports blogger reported Haren's loss in a terse Web update:

> Dodgers pitcher **Dan Haren** got roughed up Sunday afternoon against the Brewers, lasting only three innings in a 7–2 defeat. He allowed six runs—three earned—and five hits with three walks and three strike-outs. Over his last four starts covering 20⅔ innings, Haren has allowed 12 earned runs. He owns a 4.59 ERA and a 1.31 WHIP over 25 starts (143 innings).

Haren offered no excuses for losing as many games as he won. Yes, he had twinges in his hip. Sometimes he threw a pitch, came down on his front foot, and his hipbone spent a split-second grinding sideways, finding its socket. Sometimes his shoulder ached. Sometimes his elbow shot stingers up his arm, but that was nothing new. "The season's so long, there's only a few times you go out there feeling great," he told me. "Something's always sore, especially late in the year. You tough it out." He worked out in the off-season. He worked out between starts. As he got older, he cut down his bad habits until there were none left. No more fast food. No more fried food. No more dessert. By 2014, his most sumptuous meal ended with a bowl of fruit washed down with mineral water. He allowed himself one diet soda per day.

He didn't want to brag, not with a record of 10–10, but when I said there must be something he was proud of after twelve years in the big leagues, he admitted there was. "Learning how to compete on a day when I don't have my 'A' stuff," he said. "That's hard. The hitters are so tough at this level. They adapt. They adjust. If you've got a weakness, they'll feast on it. And now that it's later in my career, I struggle more. I've had a lot more bad outings, and I've found that the more you struggle, the more you need your family."

For him the one drawback of playing major league ball is the time away from his family. He doesn't complain, at least not on the record, because who's going to cry for a $10 million-a-year jock who misses his wife and kids? "I know how blessed I am, playing a game for so much money that we shouldn't ever have to worry about money." Still, he pictures Rhett and Ella's days going by while he's on charter planes or in hotels and ballparks all over the country. Even when the Dodgers played at home, his kids were asleep by the time he got back at one or two in the morning. During the school year, they were in class until just before he left for Dodger Stadium. "Some-times I can't wait for the off-season. When things are going good on the field, I like playing ball, but when I'm going bad, getting hit, I'd rather stay home."

Of all the ballplayers I've met, Haren is the most open about his insecurities. Thirty years of sportswriting had convinced me that many, if not most, great athletes, from Ty Cobb and Ted Williams to Michael Jordan, Barry Bonds, and Tiger Woods, are driven largely by grudges. *I'll prove them all wrong.* Haren's the opposite. He's all self-doubt and worry, wrapped as tightly as the quarter mile of yarn inside a baseball. His father, who had pushed him to max out his talent, couldn't help him now. Over twenty years, Dan Sr. had progressed from taskmaster to cheer-leader, but what did he know about pitching in the major leagues? Not much more than his son told him.

"When you struggle, you feel alone," Haren Jr. told me after another loss in August. "Not just batted balls. You get cursed at. You get criticized on TV, the Internet, social media. You don't want to hear it. I try to block it out. If I get hit, I'm not watching ESPN or going to baseball websites.

But then what do you do? You're just sitting in the hotel, getting lonely."

He tried Skyping his family, "but that wasn't so good. Rhett didn't like it. He's six. To him, it's just a reminder that I'm not home. He figures that if I say I'd like to be with him, I should do it. Just come home! He gets mad at me even when I'm home because he knows I'll go on a road trip soon. That's hard. I'll go to give him a hug, but he doesn't want one."

During homestands, Jessica drove their kids from Orange County to Dodger Stadium to see Daddy pitch, and the family highlights differed from the ones on *SportsCenter*. "I could pitch a no-hitter, and they'd tell me about the big foam finger they bought in the fourth inning," Haren said, laughing. "The other night, I got beat. I got booed. I came home hanging my head, but they'd had a great game. 'Daddy, we got cotton candy!'"

As of June 2014, he had spent fourteen years playing ball on Father's Day. "Baseball is *on* on the holidays. Our job's to put on a show for other families, not stay home with ours. Wherever I am on Father's Day, I look for fathers and sons in the stands, or fathers and daughters, and throw them a ball, and count the days till I'm home."

Two months later, with his spot in the Dodgers' rotation in doubt, Haren felt his career dwindling just as his children began to comprehend what he did for a living. Rhett and Ella loved to run the bases at the stadium, a privilege manager Don Mattingly allowed his players' kids after Sunday afternoon games. To them, the bases seemed a mile apart. First-grader Rhett yelled, "Go Dodgers!" and "Go Daddy!" but was still on the cusp of appreciating how singular Daddy's job was. And how much would Ella remember of the summer when she was four?

"I want to take advantage of what's left of my career, so they'll have more to remember," Haren said.

With seven starts left in the regular season, his 4.59 ERA was almost a run worse than the league average. He needed to pitch 37 more innings, about six decent starts' worth, to trigger his $10 million option for 2015. That would make each remaining outing one of the most important of his life. As much as he looked forward being home with his family, he hoped to bow out on his terms. He didn't want to be told to go home.

Meanwhile, on a 90-degree September night in Scottsdale, a boy in a wheelchair tapped a grounder toward third base under the lights at Dan Haren Field. Dan Sr., calling play-by-play, leaned into his microphone: "And there it goes . . . !"

4

★ *Cooperstown* ★

BASEBALL'S AMERICAN DADS

Cooperstown buzzes in July. It's hot and muggy, the air dotted with mosquitoes, dragonflies, and swarms of gnats, the sidewalks swarming with baseball-mad tourists. For much of the year, Cooperstown, a central New York village whose 1,900 citizens wouldn't fill a high school gym, is about as busy as the Gideon Bibles dozing in drawers in its empty hotel rooms, but in midsummer the place gets jammed like New Orleans during Mardi Gras. In July 2014, you could pretty much forget about getting a hotel room unless your name was Maddux, Glavine, Cox, La Russa, Torre, or Big Hurt.

Those names belonged to the newest Hall of Fame class. Three players and three managers, their hairlines higher and faces a little rounder than on their baseball cards, took turns addressing 48,000 starstruck fans scattered on a meadow behind the reserved seats at the Clark Sports Center. Greg Maddux, as every fan knew, was the control freak who won 355 games for four teams from 1986 to 2008. Tom Glavine, the lefty in the

Braves' brilliant Maddux-Glavine-Smoltz trio of starters in the 1990s, had been almost as good. Frank Thomas, "The Big Hurt," used to warm up by swinging a rusty length of rebar he found at the site of the old, demolished Comiskey Park; his hammer-thrower swing produced 521 homers and a .301 career batting average. During his induction speech, the mountainous Thomas spoke to his late father. "Frank Sr., I know you're watching," he said, glancing at the sky. "You always preached to me, 'You can be someone special if you really work at it.' I took that to heart, Pop. Look at us today."

Tony La Russa had the day's best line. A polymath whose teams won six pennants and three World Series, an innovator who helped bring advanced stats into major-league dugouts and often tweaked a 150-year-old tradition by batting his pitcher eighth, he said, "The more you know about baseball, the more you love it. And the more you love it, the more you want to know." While La Russa meant those lines as a sunny tribute to the game, his induction was partly clouded by memories of Mark McGwire and José Canseco, his biggest stars with the Oakland A's. When it came to their using steroids, La Russa didn't want to know. But then, baseball has always had its share of doubletalk, starting with the game's parentage.

In 1905, Albert Goodwill Spalding, a big-league

pitcher turned sporting goods tycoon, launched a commission to determine the origin of the national game. The commission was a public-relations stunt, and the fix was in. Spalding didn't care to hear that the pastime had evolved from its British precursors, cricket and rounders. As he put it, "Our good Old American game of baseball must have an American Dad." So it got one: Civil War hero Abner Doubleday, who the commission declared invented the game in Cooperstown, New York, in 1839. Never mind that Doubleday was a plebe at West Point at the time. Or that he never claimed to have invented baseball, mentioning the game only once, in passing, in a half century's worth of diaries and correspondence. The legend stuck, and the Hall of Fame opened in Cooperstown in 1939, marking the 100th anniversary of the first game that wasn't actually played there. Since then, baseball historians have rejected the myth. (One, Donald Honig, wrote that Doubleday "didn't know a baseball from a kumquat.") The Hall of Fame itself refers to "the mythical 'first game' that allegedly was played in Cooperstown." None of which kept Commissioner Bud Selig from claiming in 2010, "I really believe that Abner Doubleday is the 'Father of Baseball.'"

Some of the sport's hoariest notions carry a whiff of what Damon Runyon, the *New York American*'s baseball writer, liked to call "the phonus balonus." Philip Roth's Runyonesque sportswriter Word Smith dismissed baseball lore as "hogwash, tiny morsels of the truth so coated over with discredited legend and senile malarkey, so impacted, you might say, in the turds of time, as to rival the tales out of ancient mythology." The malarkey starts with the Cooperstown myth and often proceeds to an overly rosy view of spitting, scratching, farting, horny young men, a view that ten minutes in a clubhouse would easily cure. Fact is, with rare exceptions, most ballplayers are just guys with a heroically demanding job. Recent years have vastly raised the stakes they play for but haven't changed the players all that much. The biggest difference between today's players and those of twenty years ago, beyond their bank accounts, may be that today's major leaguers don't fraternize as much, being celebrities in their own right, with their own posses. Some might pine for the simpler days of the Big Red Machine or the Reggie Jackson Yankees until you remind them that Pete Rose prided himself on being the first singles hitter to make $100,000 a year, and Reggie made $588,000 in his best-paid Yankees season. Today, that's weight-clause money.

IN THE ARCHIVES OF THE HALL OF FAME, I tracked the career paths of the Doschers, father and son. Herm Doscher, born in 1851, ten years before Abraham Lincoln's inauguration, was a light-hitting third baseman and outfielder for the Brooklyn Atlantics of the National Association and the Troy Trojans, Chicago White Stockings, and Cleveland Blues of the National League. A sturdy fellow with a perfect part in his hair, Doscher batted .240 with no homers and 10 RBIs in 1882, his best season. He would be forgotten if not for two distinctions. After retiring, he became a scout and discovered Hall of Famer Wee Willie Keeler. And on July 2, 1902, Herm's son Jack, a left-handed pitcher, started for the Cubs, becoming the first player to follow his dad into the big leagues. Jack Doscher lost to the Philadelphia Phillies in his debut. He went 2–10 in a six-year career for the Cubs, Reds, and Brooklyn Superbas, a career distinguished solely by the fact that he was half of the first father-son duo in major-league history.

Three years passed between Jack Doscher's debut and that of James "Queenie" O'Rourke, a utility man who looked almost too small to heft his bat. Queenie broke in with the New York Highlanders—soon to become the Yankees—in 1908. He was the only son of "Orator Jim" O'Rourke, one of the pro game's pioneers, a Hall of Famer known for his erudite chatter. A Yale man with a law degree, Orator Jim enjoyed trading on-field barbs with opponents. "The exigencies of the occasion may prohibit pugilistics," he once warned a pitcher who threw near his chin.

"Subsequent developments may remove that prohibition." The Orator and his wife had seven daughters before Queenie came along in 1883. No orator, the quiet boy was a scrub who played 34 games for the 1908 Highlanders, batting .231, a midsummer double his only extra-base hit. Like Jack Doscher, he was notable only for being his father's son. Today, a life-sized statue of Orator Jim stands outside the minor-league Ballpark at Harbor Yards in their hometown of Bridgeport, Connecticut, while hardly anyone remembers Queenie.

A century ago, when some immigrant families featured ten or eleven children, single-family nines—a father and eight sons, or seven or eight brothers joined by a cousin or two—barnstormed the Northeast and Midwest, sometimes playing other bands of brothers. Fans might pay a nickel to watch. If the locals won, they might double or treble their earnings by passing the hat. In the 1930s, Walter Peckinpaugh tweaked the formula. He put together a barnstorming squad made up of second-generation players like him. His father, slick-fielding shortstop Roger Peckinpaugh, had replaced Frank Chance as the Yankees' player-manager in 1914. Son Walter, like Jack Doscher and Queenie O'Rourke, was nowhere near the player his old man was. Walter played 59 games in two seasons in the minors, batting .188. Later, when he assembled his traveling team "composed of sons of men whose names were once illustrious on the diamond," he was consciously appealing to the nostalgia that was already part of the game's appeal. According to one news account, "Peckinpaugh thinks the second-generation team would be a smart outfit and would have ample natural ability." But his tour fell apart before Peckinpaugh's boys played a single game. Baseball fans seemed willing to pay to see their heroes, but the heroes' less-talented sons? Not so much.

In the 1940s, Frederick Lieb of *The Sporting News* wondered why ballplayers' boys never seemed to measure up. Lieb had already changed the major-league rulebook by arguing, decades earlier, that a batter who socks a game-ending homer should get credit for a homer, not a single, despite the fact that his run wasn't needed to win the game. In 1920, the year the spitball was outlawed, Commissioner Landis and the team owners agreed. They adopted Lieb's proposal, and the walk-off homer was born.

A quarter century later, Lieb tackled the "generally accepted belief that baseball talent was not handed down from father to son." Why had no elite player's son made a name for himself? For one thing, Lieb wrote, professional athletes tended to be shady characters— drunkards and ruffians, "not big family men," and had no time for a catch with their sons. He wondered whether baseball skills, like Ike Davis's Jewishness, might be matrilineal. The fact that the New York Giants' George "High Pockets" Kelly was the maternal nephew of 1890s star Bill Lange made Lieb wonder whether baseball talent could be "passed down through the mother's side." (Bob Boone, a member of the first three-generation baseball family, likes that idea. "It was my mom's side that was really athletic," says Boone, whose uncle on his mother's side, George Brown, made the College Football Hall of Fame. Barry Bonds's aunt Rosie, the Olympic hurdler, is another of the often-forgotten women who have contributed genes to baseball's talent pool.) Maybe the best example of matrilineal talent is Casey Candaele, a utility man who stole 37 bases in nine seasons with the Expos, Astros, and Indians. His mother, Helen, stole 112 for the Minneapolis Millerettes of the All-American Girls Professional Baseball League in her rookie year, 1944.

Lieb saw sons rising in the '40s, starting with Dixie Walker, who hit .357 to win the National League's batting title in 1944. Walker, a crowd-pleasing Brooklyn Dodgers outfielder dubbed "The People's Cherce" by the vowel-mangling Ebbets Field faithful, was the son of Ewart "Dixie" Walker, a pitcher who went 25–31 for the Washington Senators from 1909 to 1912. Dixie Sr. begat a pair of big-league sons: batting champ Dixie, the only player to room with both Babe

Ruth and Jackie Robinson, and Harry "The Hat," another NL batting champion. The Walker boys' 2,850 hits and combined .303 average dwarfed their father's numbers, suggesting to Lieb that the generational tide might be turning. He told *Sporting News* readers to keep a lookout for minor-league batsman Dick Sisler, son of Hall of Fame first baseman George. Meanwhile, Lieb wrote, "There isn't a single case of a big league top-notcher siring a son of equal, or even near-equal, ability." Dixie and Harry Walker disproved his thesis, but Ty Cobb agreed with Lieb. Cobb had encouraged his son Tyrus Jr. to go out for tennis at Princeton. "My boy likes baseball, but appreciates he has no outstanding ability at it," said Cobb, whose own father had sent him off to pro ball with a growl: "Don't come home a failure." Tyrus Jr. had no such pressure to perform—his father, one of the nastiest competitors the game ever saw, told him to choose a game he enjoyed.

Lieb also cited the remarkable lives of Christy Mathewson and his son. Mathewson was the tall, movie star–handsome Giants hurler known as Big Six. The progenitor of the screwball, Matty was such a stalwart Christian gentleman that one of his nicknames was "The Christian Gentleman." He never pitched on Sundays but still won 372 games for the great Giants clubs of the early twentieth century, with a career ERA of 2.13. "He gripped the imagination of a country that held a hundred million people and held this grip with a firmer hold than any man of his day," wrote Grantland Rice. During World War I, Mathewson left his wife, eleven-year-old son, Christy Jr., and their dog, Polo Grounds, to enlist in the Army. He made captain, but his lungs were damaged by poison gas during a training exercise in France. Matty contracted tuberculosis and died at the age of forty-five. (Almost a century later, when Bill James developed a formula to measure players' Hall of Fame credentials, Babe Ruth led all batters with a score of 78. Mathewson led everybody with an 84.) "Christy Jr. played a little ball at Bucknell, his father's college," Lieb wrote, "but his interest turned to the air." In 1933, Army Air Corps lieutenant Mathewson Jr. was in Shanghai. He took his bride of two weeks, Margaret, for a spin in his plane. They crashed. The twenty-eight-year-old Mathewson broke both arms and lost his left leg. He clung to consciousness long enough to tell rescuers, "Look after my wife," but she was dead. Lieb picked up the story: "Young Matty had his father's heart, even if it wasn't in baseball. He learned to operate a plane with his artificial leg and served the nation well in the last war." Christy Jr. settled in Texas after World War II. He was repairing his furnace in 1946 when it exploded, burning him to death, ending the lineage of Big Six and son.

Dick Sisler, Lieb's choice to equal or eclipse his father's Hall of Fame career, didn't. He batted .276 in eight big-league seasons, making no one forget George's career mark of .340. Thinking back to his youth, Sisler *fils* recalled "going into a barber shop and hearing men whispering about me. *'That's George Sisler's boy, but he'll never be the hitter his dad was.'* They might not have been saying that, but I thought they were. I'd stay awake at night thinking about it." At least Dick had one feat even his Hall of Fame father never topped: a pennant-winning home run. On the last afternoon of the 1950 season, Dick Sisler ripped a three-run homer at Ebbets Field to win the National League pennant for the Phillies. And it was Dick Sisler who co-starred with Joe DiMaggio in an exchange that came off Ernest Hemingway's Royal Deluxe typewriter in 1951. In *The Old Man and the Sea*, Hemingway's fisherman praises the ballplayer everyone remembers from that book in the same breath as the younger Sisler.

> "The great DiMaggio is himself again . . .
> In the other league, between Brooklyn and
> Philadelphia, I must take Brooklyn. But
> then I think of Dick Sisler and those great
> drives in the old park."

The old man goes on to muse about his hero's upbringing, tying one generation to the next:

"I would like to take the great DiMaggio fishing," the old man said. "They say his father was a fisherman. Maybe he was as poor as we are and would understand."

His companion, the boy, knows about baseball fathers and sons:

"The great Sisler's father was never poor and he, the father, was playing in the Big Leagues when he was my age."

Dick Sisler went on to manage Cincinnati in 1964 and '65—the beloved Reds teams of my youth—penciling the young Frank Robinson, Pete Rose, and Tony Pérez into his lineups. Sisler's pitching staff was stocked with trivia answers. There was Joey Jay, the first Little Leaguer to make the majors, who blew out his arm and retired with precisely 99 victories and 999 strikeouts, and Ryne Duren, the nearsighted, alcoholic reliever with Coke-bottle goggles and 100 mph heat. ("I would not admire hitting against Ryne Duren," said Casey Stengel. "If he ever hit you in the head you might be in the past tense.") Southpaw Joe Nuxhall, the youngest-ever big-league player, who went on to be WLW radio's "old lefthander," joined another lefty in Sisler's bullpen: Billy McCool, whose tendency to walk the bases loaded drove my dad to distraction.

• • •

IN THE TWENTY YEARS between Dick Sisler's prime and that of the next generation, big-league clubhouses became more family-friendly. Sisler, the Walkers, Eddie Collins Jr., and other second-generation players hadn't been welcome in their fathers' locker rooms. (Collins Jr., who had 66 major-league hits to his father's 3,315, said, "I wish I could change my name to Smith. I never could be the ballplayer dad was.") A child in the beery clubhouses of the 1940s and '50s would have been as welcome as a female reporter. Then, as ballplayers began asserting themselves in the let-it-all-hang-out '70s, they began bringing their sons to work.

"My kid, Griffey's kid, Tony Pérez's kid, they had the run of the place in Cincinnati," Rose recalls. Sparky Anderson, who managed the Reds in the '70s, had one rule: "If we lost, our kids couldn't go in the clubhouse after the game. So little Griffey, Pete Jr., and them, they'd really root for us to win."

Rose ran the Reds' annual father-son game, pitching to grade schoolers Ken Griffey Jr., Pete Rose Jr., Eduardo Pérez, and the others. "Oh, they liked being out on that big field, wearing their little half-size uniforms with their names on the back," Rose remembers. "The one disadvantage those boys had was that we never got to see their games. From Little League right up through high school, their dads were playing ball every day. That's why that time at the park meant so much." When the major leaguers took the field, the boys hit in the cage under the stands. "They'd play pickle under there," Rose says. Sometimes he reminded them to watch the game's best players in action. "I'd tell my kid, look at how Joe Morgan plays second base. Watch Mike Schmidt play third. Watch *me*."

There were limits to the Reds' open-door policy. "I had a daughter, too," says Rose, "but she couldn't go on the field. She couldn't go in the clubhouse. You can understand it—naked guys walking around and all—but it's tough on a daughter to be left out. We love our girls just as much, you know."

Buddy Bell, one of Rose's successors as Cincinnati's third baseman, was the son of outfielder Gus Bell, a Reds All-Star who batted .300 with 30 homers and 105 RBI in 1953, second-best on that team to the .318, 40, and 108 posted by Ted Kluszewski. (That was a decade after Kluszewski launched the homer off Butler University's Art Cook that remains in orbit today.) Born in Pittsburgh during his dad's three-year stint with the Pirates, Buddy used to stand outside big-league locker rooms, listening for his dad's voice. By the time he grew up and made his fifth All-Star team in 1984, Buddy had proved himself as major leaguer and survivor. After collapsing with several seizures, he learned he was epileptic. One day, after tumbling out of a golf cart and breaking his nose, he checked himself into and out of a hospital, and then drove to the ballpark and doubled in his first at-bat.

By then, Buddy had two sons. "He was our idol," recalls Mike Bell, now the Diamondbacks' director of player development. "Not just for how he played, but how hard he tried to be a good dad." Buddy remembered feeling hurt when his father went on the road. He hated doing the same to his sons. "The hardest part of the game is leaving your kids behind," he said. Gus Bell often filled in for him at the boys' Little League games. "Grandpa was always there," Mike says. "We knew Dad would have been there if he could."

"You have to do as much with your kids as possible," Buddy told the *Cleveland Plain Dealer* when Mike was three and his brother, David, was five, "but no matter how you try, there is going to be a void in their lives." As a player rep, Bell was active in the players' association, which was gaining influence under union leader Marvin Miller. Bell lobbied to change team policies that kept players' kids out of clubhouses. "We don't have enough time with our children," he said. The owners had bigger battles on their hands—the reserve clause, free agency, player salaries approaching a then-shocking average of

$400,000—and so, with no fanfare, Bell helped players win the right to bring their boys to work.

"We *loved* it!" says Mike. "Taking BP, running around the field, sitting around Dad's locker. But he was strict with us, too. He made sure there was no goofing off. The clubhouse, the ballpark—this was his workplace, a respectful place."

Buddy Bell spent four seasons with Reds teams managed by Pete Rose before retiring in 1989, the year Ken Griffey Jr. broke in with the Mariners. Bell had won six Gold Gloves by then, partly by daring batters to beat him. Unlike many modern third sackers who crowd the line until half their range is in foul territory, particularly in the late innings, he often played twenty feet off the line, allowing the shortstop to cover more ground up the middle. Along with the Phillies' Schmidt, Bell was the best-fielding third baseman of his time. Upon his retirement, he had also combined with his father, Gus, for 4,337 hits, breaking the Sislers' father-son record (since topped by the Bondses' 4,821 and the Griffeys' 4,924).

In 1995, Buddy's son David was playing for the Triple-A Louisville Redbirds when sixty-six-year-old Gus Bell suffered a heart attack. Within days, the Indians called David to the majors, making Gus, Buddy, and David the game's second three-generation family. Buddy sat beside Gus in the hospital that night, listening to the radio. "David had his first big-league at-bat, and I was with Dad, listening, and he was thrilled. He died two nights later."

Buddy Bell was managing the Rockies in 2001 when David, playing third for Seattle, helped beat them with a homer. It wasn't the first time David had homered off one of his dad's pitchers. "I don't want to go through that again," Buddy said later, agonizing between team and family loyalties. He was trying to handle one of sports' most basic dilemmas: How do you treat your son if he's playing for you—or against you? Almost every dad claims he treats his kid the same as all the others. The honest ones admit how hard that can be. Forget, for a moment, the familiar sight of the coach's son batting cleanup and pitching for his dad's team. Ask yourself if you'd walk your son if he were the best player on the other team, when he was dying to hit? When his mother, relatives, and teammates were dying to see him hit? When a crucial at-bat might test his mettle, and isn't that what sports are supposed to do? A homer might build his confidence. A strikeout might toughen him up.

David Bell said homering against his dad's Rockies felt "weird. I prefer playing against someone else." On David's next trip to the plate with a game at stake, Buddy had a choice to make. Should his Rockies pitch around his son? Or challenge him? Suppose he crowded the plate— should the Rockies throw inside? How far inside?

Just enough to move him back, or do you knock your son down? Do you throw inside at butt level, the responsible way, or brush him back with something more emphatic, near the chin? What if the pitch gets away?

Buddy chose not to walk his son—or knock him down—but he hated the choice. "You look at your kid so differently . . . I wasn't sure how to handle it."

IN THE END, Buddy Bell's most lasting contribution to the game went almost unnoticed: he lobbied for a more open clubhouse.

Team policies vary. Each manager decides how porous his locker room will be. Things have tightened since 2002, when Dusty Baker's San Francisco Giants faced the Anaheim Angels in the World Series. During Game Five, Darren Baker, Dusty's three-year-old son, toddled to the plate to retrieve Kenny Lofton's bat. Darren was about to get creamed by the runner scoring from third—none other than David Bell—when the Giants' J. T. Snow swept him out of harm's way. After that, an MLB rule decreed that batboys—and girls—must be at least fourteen. Most teams, fearing liability—what if a child gets hit by a ball?—no longer allow players' kids to take grounders or batting practice on the field. Fewer boys grow up shagging flies or stepping in for an occasional pitch or two during BP, getting tips from the world's best ballplayers. "It wasn't like a formal clinic in our day," Aaron Boone says, recalling pregame practice at Veterans Stadium in Philadelphia. "It was better. Let's say you're ten years old, and you get a minute in the cage with Mike Schmidt or Pete Rose. They say, 'Get your hands a little higher.' You listen. It sinks in. There's less of that now." The golden age of being a big leaguer's son might have begun in the 1970s and ended in 2002, when Snow saved Darren Baker from a barreling Bell.

"My kids had a bat in their hands before they could walk. They had a social advantage, too," Bob Boone says. "They were raised with the game in their blood, like me. Some kids, they come up through the minors, and when they finally reach the big leagues, it knocks their socks off. 'Holy crap, there's Mike Trout!' Not my boys. Griffey Jr., Barry Bonds, same way. They didn't hope or think they belonged. They *knew*."

Brian McRae knew he belonged. His father, Hal, a Reds teammate of Rose's under Sparky Anderson, was on the road when his son was born. He never got to see Brian play a Little League or high school game. Hal barely knew how his son looked at the plate until he managed him with the 1991 Royals, becoming the fourth father (after Connie Mack, Yogi Berra, and Cal Ripken Sr.) to skipper a club with his son on the roster.

Bright-eyed, bubbly Brian took one look around

Royals Stadium and thought, "I'm home." He remembered running across the outfield turf as a five-year-old, spelunking tunnels under the stands, climbing halfway to the moon to watch his dad's team from the top row in the upper deck. "We played tape-ball games in the Royals bullpen," Brian told *Sports Illustrated*. "You'd get various hits for hitting different pieces of equipment stored in the bullpen—a double off a John Deere tractor." Later, playing backyard baseball in a Kansas City suburb, he learned to switch-hit with no help from Hal. As Brian recalled, the McRaes' backyard diamond had a short left-field fence porch. "But it ended at a mean lady's yard. She wouldn't give the ball back." A natural righty like his father, he batted left-handed to avoid the mean lady.

Ten years later, Hal found time to watch Brian play an A-ball game for the Fort Myers Royals. He was impressed to see his son switch-hitting. But Brian was slumping. After a strikeout, he trudged to the dugout. Spotting his parents in their front-row seats, he called to his father, "Will you help me?"

Hal turned to his wife. "*Now* he asks me."

AS A TEENAGER, Ken Griffey Jr. couldn't get along with his father. Ken Sr., a quick (and quick-tempered) outfielder, batted .336 for the 1976 Reds, one of the best teams ever, and hit .296

with 200 steals in a distinguished nineteen-year career. But he was no doting dad. Ken Sr. wasn't home much, and when he was, they argued. By the time "Junior" Griffey became a Cincinnati high school phenom—scouts called him the best prospect of the century—he was miserable. "My father and I were always fighting," he recalled. "It seemed like everyone was yelling at me in baseball, then I came home and everyone was yelling. I got depressed. I got angry." He considered shooting himself with his dad's gun. Instead, the seventeen-year-old Griffey downed a bottle of aspirin—277 pills, enough to kill him. His girlfriend's mother drove him to the hospital, where doctors pumped his stomach. His father rushed to the hospital, where they argued again. Ken Sr. was angry: "How *could* you?!" Junior, amazed at his dad's reaction, tore an IV from his arm and threatened to hurt himself again.

"That stopped him yelling," he said later.

It got better from there. Maybe they never had the time or inclination to sit down and talk it out, but they called a truce. Ken Sr. yelled less. Ken Jr. devoted his energies to proving he was better than any other ballplayer alive, including a once-speedy, now-gimpy, .206-hitting Reds outfielder who wasn't quite ready to retire.

In his first big-league at-bat, nineteen-year-old Ken Griffey Jr. doubled off Oakland's Dave Stewart. A year later, the Reds released his forty-year-old father. Ken Sr. signed with the Seattle Mariners, his son's team, and on the last day of August 1990, he and Junior became the first father and son ever to play in the same big-league game. They each went one-for-four in a Mariners victory. Better yet was an inning at the Big A in Anaheim two weeks later, when Ken Sr. homered. Finishing his home-run trot, he met the next batter, Ken Jr., at the plate. "That's how it's done, son," he said. Four pitches later, Junior homered—the first and probably only back-to-back father-son home runs the game will ever see.

I spoke to Ken Sr. when I was working at *Sports Illustrated*. Other writers warned me that he could be "touchy" or "surly." Maybe he'd mellowed. When we talked, he remembered his son as "an uncoordinated kid because he grew so fast and his knees always hurt. When I was playing minor-league ball in Canada and Junior was about three, he'd play Wiffle ball under the stands. When he heard my name announced, he'd climb a ledge to watch. All I could see was this little head peeking over the fence." Ken Sr. recalled the Reds' father-son games at Riverfront Stadium in Cincinnati. "He'd be so excited, he'd wake up at 6 a.m. to put on his little Reds uniform." Every Father's Day, he said, Junior gave him a bottle of Old Spice after-shave. Ken Sr. never had the heart to say he couldn't stand the stuff. Years later, he ran across seven unopened Old Spice bottles in a closet.

"I never felt overshadowed by him," Ken Sr. told me. Junior might have swatted 630 homers and driven in 1,836 runs to his 152 and 859, but dads don't give in so easy. Ken Sr. was quick to point out that his career average was a dozen points better than his son's .284. "I'm proud of him," he said, "and he always calls me on Father's Day. We talk about his kids, Trey and Taryn. I don't expect a Father's Day gift. Now that he's a dad, it's his day. But I tell Trey and Taryn to get him some Old Spice."

In 1991, the year Ken Sr. retired, his son was one of twenty-nine second-generation players in the majors. At the All-Star Game that year, they accounted for more than half the American League's starting lineup: Griffey Jr., Ripken Jr., Danny Tartabull (son of José), Sandy and Roberto Alomar (sons of Sandy). By 1997, there were thirty-two sons of big-league fathers in the majors. Their number has since leveled off. In 2014, as in 1997, thirty-two sons of big leaguers played in the majors. They included Prince Fielder, Dee Gordon, and Adam LaRoche. The Mariners' Robinson Canó was the most accomplished; his father, José, pitched six games for the 1989 Astros and named his son for Jackie Robinson. Then, as now, baseball featured more father-son links than any other major sport—more than the NFL, NBA, and NHL combined. Why? Joel Sherman of the *New York Post* posed that question to baseball men he knew. According to Sherman, "Everyone spoken to cited a modern factor for the ascendance of descendants: the removal as taboo of having children in the clubhouse. Buddy Bell said players of the 1970s demanded more time with their families."

David Laband agrees, to a degree. "Is baseball 'in the blood'? Yes. We've shown that," says Laband, chairman of the school of economics at Georgia Tech University. "But not in an obvious way. It's not genetics. Quite the opposite, in fact." In 1985, Laband and his colleague Bernard Lentz performed one of the first academic studies of what they dubbed "occupational following," the tendency of children to enter a parent's—usually a father's—line of work. It's a familiar phenomenon: from coal miners to politicians and even presidents, children have a tendency to follow the family business. Previous studies had focused on low-paying jobs; Laband and Lentz were among the first to look at pro sports. Noting that 4 percent of major leaguers in the early 1980s were the sons of major leaguers, they pointed out that such a number was a hundred times what a normal bell curve would produce. "There was clearly a powerful factor at work," says Laband, "and when you think about baseball, it makes sense. Consider the relative importance of purely physical attributes in various sports. Height, speed, strength—those are things than cannot be taught. They matter in baseball, but they matter more in football or basketball. I'd argue that the ratio of mental to physical attributes is greater in baseball than in any other major sport. That makes generational transmission more likely."

Cal Ripken Jr. told Laband about attending clinics his father ran for baseball hopefuls. "I listened to him talk," Cal Jr. said, "because I knew he'd like that. I came early to the ballpark and shagged in the outfield because I knew he'd be proud of me for doing that. And it seemed to me that his job was the best job in the whole world." Laband admits that genes make a difference: "Speed, visual acuity, quick reflexes, agility— these physical traits may form part of the legacy inherited by the son of a former standout ballplayer. But the transfer of such physical capital does not determine why a child follows in a parent's footsteps." He and Lentz have argued that early training may be "especially important in baseball, since its skills are largely learned rather than inherited. A grounder to the first baseman with runners on first and third, for example, calls for different reactions from the infielders and the runners depending on how many outs there are, the speed of the runners, the score of the game, and what inning it is. The ability to react quickly and correctly is bankable human capital."

The daily, hourly, even minute-to-minute immersion in the game that the Boones, Ripkens, and others recall—that's what Laband means when he says that many second- and third-generation players have baseball in their blood. Genes matter, but so do baseball memes. It might be accurate to say that baseball's in the house as well as the blood when the game is in the family.

There's another factor. "This may sound unscientific," Laband says, "but I believe in intestinal fortitude. Pro baseball is a hard fight you fight almost every day. Next-generation players face the same challenges their peers face, plus the burden of their names. From their first minor-league game, they're subject to special scrutiny. 'You stink! You'll never be as good as your old man!' And the better their father was, the worse the jeers are likely to be. I suspect the extra pressure makes it *harder* for baseball players' sons to succeed, at least at first. It defeats some. But if they can cope, they adapt early to the pressure-cooker environment of professional sports. By the time they reach the major leagues, they're ready in every way."

Asked why the number of second-generation players has plateaued in recent years, Laband points to the game's economics. "The money's now so huge it increases the talent pool. There are more talented athletes competing for every roster spot. That narrows the familial edge. And I suspect today's players' kids may have more affluenza—the son of a wealthy baseball player may not be as incentivized as a kid in Puerto Rico with dreams of the big leagues. I suspect we'll see fewer second- and third-generation players in the future."

No second-generation major leaguer has made the Hall of Fame. (Cal Ripken Sr. managed the Baltimore Orioles in the late '80s, but never played in the big leagues.) Griffey Jr. should be the first—a likely first-ballot inductee in 2016, the first year he's eligible. Rangers first baseman Fielder and the Mariners' Canó stood the best chance to follow him into the Hall as the 2015 season began. Prince Fielder had 288 homers, a .285 career average, and five All-Star appearances at age thirty. He missed most of 2014 after having surgery to repair herniated disks in his neck, but was Ripkenesque before that, missing only one game since 2008. A poor fielder with sinking peripheral numbers, he would need half a dozen more 25-homer seasons to make a strong run at the Hall. Canó, at thirty-two, carried a .310 career average into 2015, along with five consecutive All-Star starts and better metrics such as OPS (on-base plus slugging) and WAR (wins above replacement). Canó was on the upswing, needing four or five strong seasons to make his case for induction.

For now the lone father-son duo in the Hall is a pair of executives, Larry and Lee MacPhail, who ran three teams between them and reached

Cooperstown in 1978 and 1998, respectively. Of today's players, Fielder's dad (Cecil), Scott Van Slyke's (Andy), and Kyle Drabek's (Doug) were stars, but only Tony Gwynn Jr.'s was a Hall of Famer. The younger Gwynn, a thirty-two-year-old outfielder, had a .238 career average through 2014, so Griffey—assuming he's inducted in 2016—stands to be the only second-generation Hall of Fame player for another decade or more.

ON THE FIRST Hall of Fame induction day in 1939, Ruth and Cobb's speeches were a paragraph each. Over time, as the Hall grew in importance, the speeches got longer—even tight-lipped Steve Carlton went on for fifteen minutes. Many inductees have shared the honor with their dads.

Mickey Mantle, enshrined in 1974, told how his father, a zinc miner known as Mutt, "named me after a Hall of Famer, Mickey Cochrane." According to family lore, Mutt Mantle was heartbroken when his son reached for his baby bottle instead of the baseball his dad was waving at him. Mickey was twelve hours old. "My father used to say that it seemed to him like he died in the winter, until the time baseball came around again. My first lullaby was the radio broadcast of a ballgame. One night, Mama says, I woke up . . . she pleaded with Dad to 'cut off that contraption' and let me sleep. 'You got Mickey wrong, hon,' Dad said. 'I don't blame him for screaming. He knew the situation called for a bunt instead of hitting away.'" Mantle recalled how his father would hurry home from backbreaking eight-hour shifts in the mine, "and after we milked the cows we would play ball till dark. I don't know how he kept doing it."

Bill Mazeroski, the hero of the Pirates' 1960 World Series victory, was another miner's son. Recalling Lew Mazeroski, who lost a foot in a coal-mining accident, Bill told a Cooperstown crowd, "When I was old enough to walk, Dad took me in the backyard and taught me baseball. He wanted to make his dream come true through me."

Of all the tributes Hall of Famers paid to their dads, few have matched Phil Niekro's. Born in 1939, the king of knuckleballers grew up when major-league baseball was a good job but not yet a millionaire's career. Boys played because they enjoyed the game, or were better at it than other boys, or wanted to be like Dad. Niekro, known as Knucksie for the knuckleball his dad taught him, reached the majors despite throwing no harder than 85 miles an hour, "and that was with the wind behind me." He went on to win 318 games, retiring at the age of forty-eight with a career ERA of 3.35. On the day of his Hall of Fame induction in 1997, a red carnation tucked into his gray lapel, he thanked everyone in sight, including brother Joe, another knuckleballer, who won 221 big-league games. (The Niekro brothers' total of 539 victories is another of those records that won't be broken.) Then he spoke of his father, Phil Sr., yet another miner, a semipro pitcher who breathed coal dust on the job for half a century, sweated coal-black droplets after work, and played ball on his few days off.

"There's one man that's not here," Phil Niekro said at Cooperstown in 1997. "A man that taught me how to catch a fish, how to put a worm on the hook. He taught me how to play pinochle, took me to church, always had time for his family, didn't make a whole lot of money . . . and always told me, 'Son, if you want to earn an honest day's dollar, you've got to put in an honest day's work.' I have tried to do that my whole life, every time I put that major-league baseball uniform on . . . When I walked onto the field and the umpire dusted off home plate—he'd look at me and say, 'Play ball, son. Play ball.'"

Closing his speech, Niekro pictured his long-dead father taking the mound one last time, surrounded by teammates whose names his son remembered. "If we could go back sixty years to that little ball field back in Blaine, Ohio, there'd probably be a game going on," Niekro said. "Some coal miners playing some other coal miners. And as my dad would take the field, the lineup would probably sound something like this . . . First base would be Chester Casper; second base, Frank Merckowski; shortstop, Charlie Pocis;

third base, Cookie Terhole; left field, Ziggy Berlinski; center field, Walter Barbac; right field, Pete Sabbath; catching, Stush Maholski; and in the bullpen, Lefty Yurk. And as Clarence Nitsell dusts off home plate, about right now, I say to you, Dad, 'Play ball, Dad. Play ball.' "

5

★ *Drilling the Muscle* ★

THREE GENERATIONS OF BOONES

Ray Boone drove to work with his son, Bob, clambering around the seat beside him. Without a seat belt, of course. It was 1953. The boy reached for the steering wheel, pretending to help his dad drive, then scrambled to the passenger window for a breath of the lazy, faintly fishy breeze off Lake Erie. Five-year-old Bob watched an iceman use tongs to yank a block of ice from his truck and drop the steaming, doghouse-sized block on the curb outside a diner.

Ray parked on the street outside Cleveland Municipal Stadium. He led his boy to the only gate that was open three hours before game time, a turnstile manned by a sleepy-eyed attendant. Ray greeted the man, who waved him through with a flourish. Like anyone who had anything to do with baseball in Cleveland, the attendant knew the Indians' shortstop, a U.S. Navy veteran beloved for his war service if not for his spotty fielding and unreliable arm at shortstop. Ray always said he was a California boy, unaccustomed to the chilly winds that came off the lake, numbing his fingers and wafting his throws past first baseman Luke Easter.

Bob knew nothing of his dad's fielding troubles. "All I knew was that there was something special about this giant ballpark where my dad worked," he remembers. "And that thousands of people came to see him play."

Around the dinner table, where baseball was the only topic of conversation, Ray didn't mention throwing a ball away and getting booed. He didn't mention trade rumors. He talked about his double-play partner, Bobby Ávila, and Indians sluggers Larry Doby and Al Rosen, and the Tribe's "Big Four" rotation of Bob Feller, Bob Lemon, Mike García, and Early Wynn. "And he talked about his hero," Bob recalls. "Ted Williams."

Ray Boone, born in 1923, was the son of a lather, a woodworker who built walls on construction sites. Ray played high school ball at San Diego's Herbert Hoover High, where Ted Williams had blazed a trail five years ahead of him. By the time Ray reached the majors, the Splendid Splinter had led the American League in homers three times, batted .406 in a season, won an MVP award, and been robbed of two others, despite losing three full seasons to military service in World War II—all before turning thirty.

Ray took a more workmanlike path. After a stint in the Navy and four solid seasons in the minors, he joined player-manager Lou Boudreau's Indians in September of '48. Teammates called the rookie "Ike" for his resemblance to General Eisenhower. The twenty-five-year-old Boone batted once in that year's World Series—Warren Spahn struck him out—as Cleveland won its first Series since 1920. Ray soon settled in as the club's shortstop, hitting just enough to make fans forgive his miscues in the field. But when the Indians finished two games back of the Yankees in 1952, some blamed Boone's league-leading 33 errors. "Many people in Cleveland think we ought to get rid of him," said Indians general manager Hank Greenberg. "It's easy to see that a player has had a bad season. It isn't so easy to find a fellow who is certain to do better."

Over breakfast, over supper, or driving to the ballpark with his son Bob, Ray made baseball sound like the best job a fellow could have. Ray was proud, even a little surprised, to earn $12,000 a year, equal to about $100,000 in 2014 dollars, for playing Ted Williams's game.

As the '53 season began, Williams was flying Marine Corps jets in combat seven thousand miles away. The Splinter, true to his spit-in-your-eye disposition, had initially griped about being called up to serve in Korea. He was thirty-three years old—in midcareer. Why him? Out of five hundred major-league players, fewer than a hundred were drafted to serve in Korea. Why should he risk his neck again, a decade after losing three seasons to World War II?

Because you're such a splendid fighter pilot, the Marine Corps told him. Williams went on to win three Air Medals, flying thirty-eight combat missions over Korea, often as wingman for future astronaut John Glenn.

Ray told his son about Williams's heroics back in 1941. Going into a season-ending doubleheader, his average stood at .39955, which rounded to .400. Williams could have sat out the last day, as hitters from Ty Cobb in 1910 to Jose Reyes in 2011 have done to win batting titles. Instead, he played both games. "If I'm going to be a .400 hitter, I want more than my toenails on the line," he said. Williams went six-for-eight that day. His last hit, which lifted his average to .406, caromed off a loudspeaker atop the right-field fence and bounced back into play for a double.

Ray talked about playing against Williams before the Korean War. As the Indians' shortstop, he had to be ready to move to the right side of the infield if manager Boudreau put on the Williams Shift. The practice of shifting fielders to foil left-handed pull hitters dates back to the 1920s, when opponents overloaded the right side against the Cubs' Cy Williams, but its modern incarnation was Boudreau's brainchild. His Indians tried it in 1946 to stop Williams, or at least get under his skin. The first time he saw the shift, he stepped out of the batter's box and laughed. One newsman pointed out the ploy's weak link: "Boudreau forgot to post a fielder in the right-field bleachers." Yet the shift worked. Cleveland's fielders turned so many hot grounders and liners into outs that other teams tried the same trick against Williams, until he finally closed his stance and began slapping balls to left and left-center. By the time Ray Boone came up in '48, the Indians weren't using the Williams Shift nearly as much as they used to. Defensive shifting fell out of fashion for sixty years, until advanced metrics—data revealing where each batter tends to hit every variety of pitch on every count—brought shifting back to bedevil millennial hitters like the Mets' Ike Davis.

In 1953, less than a year after telling reporters how much he liked Ray Boone, general manager Greenberg traded him to Detroit. Tigers manager Fred Hutchinson made Boone a third baseman, a move that took some of the defensive pressure off the young infielder, who became a fan favorite and two-time All-Star. In 1955, Boone and Boston's Jackie Jensen tied for the AL RBI crown with 116. A year later, Boone batted .308 with 25 homers.

"Dad loved Detroit. Me too," Bob says. "I got to watch him and see all the greats: Williams, Mickey Mantle, Yogi Berra. Then he got traded to the White Sox. We had to move again, but I didn't mind. They had a pretty open clubhouse, especially for that time. I was ten, but they let me work out with them. I was out there taking grounders in one of Nellie Fox's extra jerseys, number 2. It was big on me, but not huge—neither was he." Second baseman Fox, the Sox' "Mighty Mite," teamed with shortstop Luis Aparicio while Ray Boone played first base. At thirty-four, Boone had lost a step. His calcified knees ached. He hobbled up and down the stairs at home. He retired two years later with a .275 career average, 151 homers and an unsightly 218 errors.

Boone wanted to stay in the game. He signed on as a scout for the Red Sox and spent the next thirty years driving from diamond to diamond around San Diego, sometimes ranging to other southwestern towns as far afield as Phoenix. He signed future major leaguers including Marty Barrett, Sam Horn, Phil Plantier, and a six-foot-five Arizona kid with a heavy fastball and a father-son story of his own.

"I WAS NINETEEN, FULL OF BEANS, and full of myself," Curt Schilling told me. Even as a junior-college pitcher, Schilling had a dash of Ted Williams in him. He was a gamer. He didn't much care what you thought of him. He would make his own way to a sort of immortality—in Schilling's case, a tortuous path from fireballing head case to a sore arm and shoulder surgery. The surgery revived his career. It added a couple ticks to his fastball, leading to back-to-back 20-win seasons and two World Series titles, including a pivotal role in the 2004 postseason, when he helped pace the curse-reversing Red Sox past the Yankees and Cardinals while pitching with a cadaver's tendon holding his right ankle together. The bloodstained sock Schilling wore that October can now be viewed at the Hall of Fame —an outcome that might have made Schilling laugh when he was a chubby, cheeky teenager with a Red Sox scout in his kitchen.

"Ray Boone wanted to sign me," Schilling remembered. "He was offering a $15,000 bonus. I wanted more." Ray was sixty-two, balding on top, and gray at the temples, 350 miles from home, his knees worse than ever. He had a hard time climbing the single step from the porch to the Schillings' living room. And he didn't seem all that eager to sign Curt Schilling. He had his savings and his pension. His son Bob, the kid who'd taken grounders in Nellie Fox's jersey, was now a big-league veteran making $850,000 a year. So Ray didn't need to sign a lumbering junior-college nobody with a strong arm and an ego to match. But he liked Schilling's size, his plus fastball, and his screw-you attitude. And after more than thirty years of scouting, he figured he knew how to get a deal done. It starts with the player's father.

Cliff Schilling was a military man, a twenty-two-year Army veteran. "When I had a jerk for a high school coach," Curt recalled, "my dad told me to say, 'Yes sir,' even when the guy was wrong. 'Don't expect fairness—that's not real life,' he said. 'Take what you're given. Do your best and get stronger.' " A heavy smoker, Cliff Schilling bounced from the Army to night-desk duty at a Ramada Inn, sneaking cigarettes even after doctors told him he had lung cancer and skin cancer. At one point, after an operation left a small hole in the bridge of his nose, he grossed his son out by blowing cigarette smoke through the hole. "He thought that was hilarious."

Cliff urged his son to sign with Ray Boone. Curt wasn't sure. "He offered me a $15,000 bonus. I said, 'Can we negotiate?' And he said no."

Ray was an old hand at this. He knew $15,000 represented a small fortune to the Schillings. He knew it was more than Cliff made in a year at the Ramada Inn. "Curt," he said, "if you're as good as I think you are, fifteen thousand is going to be meal money in three or four years. But if you're going to jerk me around over the bonus, I'm going home."

Schilling said, "Gimme the contract." He signed.

Two years later, in 1988, Cliff Schilling died and Curt made his major-league debut. "I took my first big-league paycheck to the bank. Six thousand dollars! I cashed it, all in twenty-dollar bills, and threw them on the bed in my hotel room and said, 'Dad, you were right!' "

Schilling kept his father in mind as he went from sore-armed hothead to two-time World Series hero. He told friends, teammates, and even reporters about his dad. When he wished they could share a moment, he told Cliff about it inside his head. And for the next twenty years, whenever Curt started a game, he left a ticket at the will-call window in Clifford Schilling's name.

SCHILLING WAS RAY BOONE'S TOP SIGNEE, but not his first All-Star. "That would be me," says Bob, who broke in with the last-place Phillies in 1972. Like his father (and, later, his sons), Bob Boone started out as an infielder. In the minors, he played third base beside a bonus-baby shortstop named Mike Schmidt. "I felt old. I was twenty-three and still in Double-A ball," Bob remembers. The big club had an opening at catcher, a position he disdained. "You catch because you have to, not because you want to." He figured he had to, or risk aging out of his shot at the big leagues. He had the size for it—at six foot two and 195 pounds, he was bigger than his father. His knees were free of the calcium deposits that had turned Ray's knees to chalk, and it turned out he had a catcher's head, too.

Bob Boone had a knack for thinking two or three pitches in advance. He'd block the plate against a charging runner, bark at a strike-zone-squeezing umpire, bully a pitcher into throwing the right pitch. Rejecting the then-common belief that weight lifting made ballplayers muscle-bound, Bob worked out in a gym all winter and reported to spring training at his fighting weight. He became the most durable receiver of his time, catching 130-plus games a year as the Phillies rose from doormats to pennant contenders. An All-Star in 1976, '78, '79, and '83, he batted around .275 with 60 RBIs year after year, winning a slew of Gold Gloves while "bullying, babying, and whatever-it-tooking" a pitching staff that featured surly ace Steve Carlton, veterans Jim Kaat and Jim Lonborg, and flaky closer Tug McGraw. Thirty years later, Ray Boone's son is justly proud of his nineteen-year major-league career. What annoys him is being remembered for a pop-up that bounced off his mitt.

It happened in the 1980 World Series. The Phils, whose hometown fans often called them the Phutile Phillies, were going for the first championship in franchise history. Since the World Series began in 1903, the Philadelphia club was the only member of the majors' "Original Sixteen" to be oh-for-forever. As of 1980, the Phillies hadn't even won a World Series game since 1915. But they beat George Brett and the Kansas City Royals three times in the first five games of the 1980 Series. Coming home to Veterans Stadium for Game Six, they were poised to reverse a curse of their own.

Top of the ninth: Philadelphia 4, Kansas City 1. With one out, the Royals load the bases against screwballer Tug McGraw. Frank White lifts a foul pop toward the Phillies' dugout. Boone peels off his mask and gives chase. First baseman Pete Rose, late to the play, hesitates. Boone expects Rose to take charge. "The catcher is supposed to wait till the first baseman calls him off," he recalls today. "The ball's coming down and I'm thinking, 'Where's Rose?' "

Boone stabs for the ball. It bounces off his mitt. The baseball hangs in midair for an instant. The Royals have new life while Phillies fans flash back to the infamous Phold of '64, when the Phils lost ten in a row to blow a six-and-a-half-game lead in the final two weeks, a swoon triggered when the Reds' Chico Ruiz stole home to beat them 1–0. ("That play busted our humps," said Dick Allen.) After that, Philadelphians blamed the club's losing on what they called the Curse of Chico Ruiz. Will this mix-up be remembered as the Curse of Bob Boone?

No—Rose snags the ball in midair. Two outs. Next, with Willie Wilson looking for a screwball, catcher Boone and closer McGraw cross him up with a fastball for strike three. McGraw lifts his arms, setting off a celebration that leads to a parade down Broad Street in which 800,000 fans salute their first-ever champions, regular-season and World Series MVP Mike Schmidt, Carlton, and McGraw as well as "Charlie Hustle" Rose and Boone, the last two of whom are still needling each other about one of the most famous plays in Phillies history.

"Charlie Hustle, my ass," Boone says, thirty-five years after the day. "I was the one hustling on that ball. Pete was just late enough to catch it."

"I seem to remember one of us caught it. I think it was me," Rose counters. Recalling his Philadelphia years with pugnacious pride, he points out that the winless Phils won a World Series and two National League pennants in his five seasons with them. They made the playoffs three times; he made the NL All-Star team four times. "I had a hell of a time in Philly. You know why I went there in the first place? One reason was the clubhouse. They had a real family-friendly clubhouse."

BRET BOONE WAS ELEVEN the year his dad's team won the 1980 World Series. His brother Aaron was seven. Along with the sons of Pete Rose, Greg "The Bull" Luzinski, and other Phillies, they thought of manager Dallas Green's clubhouse at Veterans Stadium as a second home. Bret and Aaron had their own locker, chock-full of toys and mini-uniforms. They bombed around the clubhouse riding Bret's Big Wheel—a plastic tricycle—veering around folding chairs, stools, discarded towels, and jockstraps. During batting practice, they ran onto the field to take grounders, ducking sizzling liners off the bats of Schmidt and Luzinski, whose quicksilver swing once produced a line drive the third baseman jumped for as the ball rose and cleared the left-field fence for a homer.

Ryan Luzinski, the Baby Bull, would spend eight years in the minors, but he never got a major league at-bat. Pete Rose Jr. would spend twenty-one seasons in the minors, a rugged apprenticeship that got him a handful of at-bats in the big leagues with the 1997 Reds. By then, his dad was a pariah, banned indefinitely for betting on ballgames while managing the Reds. Pete Jr., known as Petey, had a pair of singles in his 14 major league at-bats, compared to his dad's 4,256 base hits. But in the early '80s, with Pete Rose Jr., Ryan Luzinski, the Boone boys, and other players' kids racing around Veterans Stadium, there was no telling which kid had big-league potential.

"We knew who was the cockiest, though," Rose says. "Boone's boy was the same age as mine, but he acted like a hotshot. The other players' kids are out there shagging flies before the game, trying not to get hit in the head, and Bret's hot-doggin' it, catching the ball behind his back. I told my son, 'That's not the way. You should prove yourself before you show off, and once you prove yourself, you don't have to show off.'"

There might have been other kids, like Petey

Rose, who wanted to play major-league ball as much as Bret Boone, but it's safe to say nobody expected it more. Like Mickey Mantle and Ike Davis, he had a toy bat and ball in his hands while he was still in diapers. Unlike them and other toddlers, Bret was walking when he was six months old, jumping off diving boards at seven months, brandishing a cut-down wooden bat as soon as he could toddle. "Bret did things that were spooky," his father says. "He could hit a ball over our house when he was a year old. That's not a joke—one year old. By the time he was seven or eight, he was three years ahead of other kids his age."

Bob credits genetics—athletic talent on both sides of the family—for his first son's precocity. But nurture played its role as well. Bret's father and grandfather watched over his first swings. As he grew and began taking cuts at the Vet, Schmidt, Luzinski, Allen, Rose, and other Phillies took an interest. Nothing formal, but if Dick Allen says, "Keep your weight back," a boy tends to take the tip. He tends to start out with big-league technique, bypassing bad habits. Bob Boone calls it "drilling the muscle." Talent plus technique plus repetition equals success. "Talent's the raw material you start with," says Boone. "Add years of muscle memory, and that kid's going to max out."

Cal Ripken Jr. learned similar lessons. His

father spent thirteen years managing in the Orioles' minor-league system, often taking young Cal to the park with him. "I went so I could be alone with him on the drive and back," Ripken Jr. told sportswriter Jack Elkin. After a game, while Cal Sr. did his managerial paperwork, filling out reports for the big club, they compared notes. "I'd say, 'Doug DeCinces told me this is the way to field a grounder,' and I'd show my father. He agreed, so I made sure to talk to DeCinces again. If he disagreed with something I'd learned, I wouldn't go back to that guy."

Bret and Aaron Boone's boyhood was an experiment in baseball immersion. The Boones seemed immune to burnout or boredom with the game. "My grandfather and I watched ballgames on TV while Aaron was crawling around, absorbing that 'it' factor. Whatever it was, we got it in our bones," Bret says.

"I was born in '73, my dad's first full season in the majors," says Aaron. "He retired my first year in high school, so baseball was the only life I knew. The best childhood ever." Aaron tagged along with big brother Bret, played ball with older boys, piled into the family car for the half-hour drive from their home in Medford, New Jersey, to the stadium in Philadelphia. "Our playground," he calls it. "We got to hit and shag. Of course, you had to know when to disappear. That was Dad's word. After BP, when it's getting close to game time, little boys disappear. We'd change out of our little Phillies unis, put our school clothes back on, and sit with Mom in the stands. Or stay in our unis and watch the game with the grounds crew."

At home, meals featured meat and potatoes and one other staple. "Did we talk about baseball? Did our lives revolve around baseball?" Bob asks. "There was nothing else. Put me, my dad, and my sons at a table, we're not going to talk about modern art."

When Bob was on the road, Grandpa Ray sat at the head of the table, dispensing old-school wisdom. "He was always comparing his time to the modern era, and not very flatteringly," Aaron says. "Bret and I liked to get him going. We'd say, 'Grandpa, tell us again how much better it used to be!' He told his old Ted Williams stories, this legendary figure from the same sandlots he grew up on. Those stories filled our house."

"Baseball is one big habit," Bob says. "It's the habit my dad gave me, and we both passed it on to my sons."

When Bret Boone was three, he announced that he was going to be a big leaguer. Bob recalls thinking, "That would make us a trivia question." It would make Ray, Bob, and Bret Boone the first three-generation major-league trio. Bret went on to set records at El Dorado High School in Orange County, California, while hot-dogging his way through puberty. Another local high school star,

Jim Campanis, son of Dodgers GM Al Campanis, held a keg party in his parents' house that year. Bret, a year or two younger than Jim and his friends, crashed the kegger. Campanis would recall "seeing this preppy-looking kid and thinking, 'What's *he* doing here?'" They became friends, and Campanis began to think Bret Boone could do just about anything he pleased.

After batting .500 in his senior season at El Dorado High, Bret expected to be a first-round selection in the 1987 amateur draft. Instead, he went to the Minnesota Twins in the twenty-eighth round. There were rumors that scouts didn't like his size, which was smallish, or his attitude, which was anything but. He spurned the Twins' offer and enrolled at the University of Southern California, where one report described him as "a helmet-throwing terror." Angry and overconfident—that was Bret's rep among pro scouts. A head case: the kind of player whose moods might ruin whatever talent he had. He was small, too. At five foot ten and 170 pounds, Bret Boone looked shrimpy beside his six-foot-two, 210-pound father. He was even smaller and lighter than his grandfather. One scouting report noted his "average speed, average arm strength, and average big-league power." According to another scout, "His hitting is suspect. He's got kind of a long swing, he's getting a lot of attention because of his name." Not enough attention to suit Bret, though. After three banner seasons at USC, he expected to be a first-round, big-bonus choice in the 1990 amateur draft. Florida high schooler Chipper Jones went first. Then, while the Boones seethed, 131 players went before the Seattle Mariners selected Bret in the fifth round. He was crushed. He was angry.

He used his fury as fuel. "I was going to prove 'em wrong." Prove *who* was wrong? "Everybody." Every scout and every team, including the Mariners, who had passed him over four times before using that fifth-round choice on him.

His father and grandfather agreed that Bret got screwed. Bob, for one, had tolerated his moody son's tantrums out of love and belief in his talent. Where some saw a Bret as a future "Quad-A" player, the kind who excels at the Triple-A level but never makes it in the majors, Bob saw his firstborn as a high-strung thoroughbred, his talent untamed but unlimited. "Bret was the extrovert, the interesting one of us." Ray, too, took his grandson's side. "There's no doubt he'll play in the big leagues," he told *USA Today*. But few of Ray's fellow scouts shared his opinion. Even Woody Woodward, the Seattle GM, had his doubts. Bret Boone, Woodward admitted, "has question marks on him defensively." So why draft him? On that point, Woodward deferred to Mariners scouting director Roger Jongewaard, who mentioned Bret's college stats and a quality that was harder to measure.

"Bret Boone," said Jongewaard, "is the most self-confident player I ever scouted."

Bret sped through the minors, batting .290 with occasional power and decent defense at second base. In 1991, *Baseball America* named him the ninety-ninth-best prospect in the minors, behind Jones, Mike Mussina, Jeff Bagwell, and dozens of guys nobody would ever hear of. Two years later, after batting .314 with 13 homers and 73 RBIs for the Triple-A Calgary Cannons, he crept up to ninety-seventh on the list. At this rate, he'd be retired before he caught up to Bagwell and the other big-time prospects.

"Oh, I was pissed," he says.

That was the year he ran into Jim Campanis again. Campanis, whose kegger the underage Bret had crashed, started his minor-league career a year ahead of him. He was now catching for the Jacksonville Suns, the Mariners' Double-A farm club. Reporters expected Campanis to be the first third-generation player to make the major leagues. Jim's father had been a scrub for the Dodgers, Royals, and Pirates from 1966 to 1973; his grandfather, Al, played briefly for the Brooklyn Dodgers, going two-for-twenty in 1943. Both of the elder Campanises went on to front-office careers. (Al, the scout who discovered Sandy Koufax, lost his job as the Dodgers' GM after telling *Nightline*'s Ted Koppel in 1987 that blacks might lack "the necessities" to become managers or club executives.) Now minor leaguer Jim greeted his former high school teammate with a dare.

"I'm going to make the Show before you," he said. Jim's dad and granddad had combined for four big-league home runs and nine RBIs to Ray and Bob Boone's 256 homers and 1,562 RBIs, but if Jim Jr. played a big-league inning before Bret, the Campanises would go into the record books.

Bret said, "Wanna bet?"

"I'll bet you a car."

Bret gave that some thought. "Well, I'm not driving some Pinto."

"A BMW."

"You're on."

August 1992. The last-place Mariners wanted help at second base. Harold Reynolds was slowing down. Two years after rookie Ken Griffey Jr. joined his father in Seattle's outfield, general manager Woodward had another feel-good story in the works. The Mariners were calling Bret Boone to the majors.

It made Bret mad. "Suddenly, I've got camera crews following me off the Triple-A field. Not because of me, because of my dad and his dad. So I'm thinking, 'Screw them.'" Echoing Barry Bonds and Griffey Jr., he claimed his parentage had nothing to do with who he was.

Bret Boone arrived in Seattle chin-first, with his

hat on backward Griffey-style, lampblack under his eyes, a pile of Hillerich & Bradsby lumber slung over his shoulder. He had an uppercut swing and an attitude that wouldn't stop. Years later, asked to describe himself upon his arrival in Seattle, he says, "I was a snot-nosed kid, but *focused*. I had a lofty opinion of myself as a player, and the third-generation thing meant nothing to me. 'Screw that, I'm here to prove myself.'"

He stepped in for Reynolds and struggled, batting only .194 the last month of the season, with four home runs to suggest how hard he was swinging for the fences. And the car Jim Campanis now owed him? His old buddy and rival sent him a two-inch-long Hot Wheels BMW.

A year later, in one of the worst deals of GM Woodward's tenure, the Mariners traded twenty-four-year-old Boone and starter Erik Hanson to the Reds for reliever Bobby Ayala and catcher Dan Wilson. Bret Boone became a star in Cincinnati, smacking 24 homers with 95 RBIs in 1998 while winning the first of four Gold Gloves—an extra "screw you" to Woodward and everyone else who doubted his defense. Three years later, after Woodward's successor, Pat Gillick, brought him back to Seattle as a free agent for $8 million a year, Bret had an even better season. Playing Gold Glove–caliber second base, he batted .331, smacked 37 homers, and led the league in RBIs for a Mariners club that went

116–46 in its best season ever. No team in major league history has won more games in a season. "That year was magic," he recalls. "A whole season without a slump, for me or the team." Seattle's lineup boasted Boone as well as another third-generation player, third baseman David Bell, plus first baseman John Olerud, DH Edgar Martínez, and a newcomer from Japan, Ichiro Suzuki, who won the American League MVP award. Yet it was Boone who set the tone. The other Mariners called him their drummer. He'd roll into the clubhouse and say, "I'm here, we can play the game now." He thinks he deserved the MVP award over Suzuki, and he's probably right. (Ichiro batted .350, with eight homers, 69 RBIs, 56 steals, and seven wins above replacement; Boone hit .331, with 37 homers, 141 RBIs, five steals, 9.2 wins above replacement.) But there were rumors that his surge in power, from a high of 24 home runs to a four-year run that began that season—37 homers, then 24, 35, and another 24—owed more to chemistry than grit. José Canseco, who outed his old friend and teammate Mark McGwire in his 2005 book *Juiced*, claimed that Bret was a juicer too.

"I *was* a substance abuser. My substance was alcohol," Boone says now.

In 2005, he was thirty-six years old, fighting age and injuries that included bum knees like his father's and grandfather's. He was brooding, too, his mind racing as usual but now mulling numbers he hated to contemplate: a .221 average in 2005, 110 points worse than his career year only four seasons past. Two twenty-one with seven home runs. His dad had batted .295 at age forty while catching 122 games!

Bret was too proud to keep watching video with coaches and teammates, seeing himself striking out, stinking it up. Drinking eased the sting. A couple of postgame beers became a six-pack or two. One day that off-season, he crashed a golf cart at Shadow Creek, Steve Wynn's exclusive course in Las Vegas. Later that day, reportedly soused, he tumbled off a bar stool in the clubhouse.

"I'd been so blessed to play fourteen years in the big leagues," he says. "And then it starts to go away. Your whole life you're Bret Boone, the second baseman, and now you have to start thinking about life after baseball. So who are you?" He hoped to put off that reckoning, at least for another year. In the winter of 2005–06, he changed his diet from beer and more beer to "fish and steamed vegetables." He worked out twice a day and reported to the Mets' spring-training camp in the best shape he'd been in since 2001. It lasted three days. "I was rusty. My knees hurt." He announced his retirement. A couple hours later, his cell phone rang.

Bob couldn't believe the news. "Tell me it's

April Fool's Day," he said. Bret told his father it was true: he was quitting. After they said goodbye, he wept all the way to the airport.

Two years later, he tried again. "I wasn't ready to walk away. It's *hard* to walk away," he says. "What if you had another good year in you?" Again he spent an off-season eating perfectly, pumping iron, hitting thousands of line drives in indoor batting cages. Again he reported to spring training, this time with the Washington Nationals. General manager Jim Bowden liked what he saw. "You can help us," he said. "Are you willing to go to the minors, work on your swing till I call you?"

"Hell yes."

He reported to the Columbus Clippers of the Triple-A International League, where the only thirty-nine-year-old Clipper proved he could still pick it at second and hit enough to help the Nationals, at least in a utility role. He was batting .261 for Columbus when Bowden called to see how he was feeling.

Boone said, "Jim, I want to be honest with you. I've worked my butt off, but I'm a shell of my old self. I can't play every day. I could give you four days a week, maybe hit .260 with 10 or 12 home runs."

"I'll take it," Bowden said.

Bret spent a long night weighing Bowden's offer. How much could he help the Washington

Nationals in 2008? "They were gonna lose a hundred games," he says. He hated losing almost as much as he hated striking out. "I thought, 'In my heyday, at my best, the game was *so hard*.' You fight every day to get a hit or two and field your position, and it's still a lot of humble pie. I walked away too early the first time, but that spring I got in the best shape, gave it the best I had left." And it wasn't enough. He had a keen sense of how he looked in the field and at bat—not to fans, but to baseball men like Bowden and Bob Boone. "I didn't want to stink." He called Bowden back and said thanks, but no thanks. He told his father he was retiring again, and this time Bob wasn't surprised. Better now than the first time, when he wasn't quite sure. Now, at least, Bret was confident he'd given the game his best, last shot.

Like Ray before him, Bob had been through the same tunnel himself, though he'd staved off retirement until he was forty-two. Fans may think retiring players relish the thought of spending more time with friends and family, skipping days or weeks in the gym, gaining a few pounds, spending summer Sundays on the golf course. And they do. Even so, retiring can feel like stepping off a cliff. It's daunting even to those who love the game and find a way to stay in it, whether as a scout like Ray Boone, a manager like Bob, who went on to manage the Royals and Reds, or a TV talker like Schilling. After twenty-five or thirty years of playing baseball for a living, the next step can't help but feel like a plunge.

Bret Boone retired for the second and last time in 2008, with a .266 career average, 252 home runs, and 1,021 RBIs. That left one Boone in the majors.

AARON BOONE STOOD SIX FOOT TWO and tipped the scale in the Cleveland Indians' clubhouse at 195. Four years younger than Bret, he was four inches taller and fifteen pounds heavier, darker of hair and eye, nowhere near as cocky, and not quite as good. Aaron was always the kid brother. "When we were little, Bret let me tag along, so I grew up playing ball with older boys." A third-round selection in the 1994 amateur draft (Nomar Garciaparra and Paul Konerko went in the first round), Aaron broke in with the 1997 Reds with none of the fanfare attending Bret's debut five years earlier.

"I was a little quieter, more under the radar," he says. Still, he was keen to prove himself. As tight as they were, the ballplaying Boones shared a drive to make their own names. When Bret came to the majors, he didn't want to hear about "the three-generation thing." When Aaron's turn came, he had to prove he was more than Bob Boone's son or Bret's little brother. "We were crazy about each other, but we're competitive guys," Aaron says. That could lead to one-upmanship in the batting cage, on the golf course, over the dinner table, or on the phone. When they disagreed about baseball, sparks flew, though most of the heat came from Bob and Bret. Aaron was less opinionated, more of a listener.

Settling in at third base for the Reds, he batted between .280 and .294 for three seasons, with 12 to 14 homers per year, practically defining good-but-not-great. In 2002, he tried swinging harder, with more of an uppercut, like Bret. Sacrificing batting average for power, Aaron socked 26 homers in 2002 and made the National League All-Star team in 2003. Seventy-nine-year-old Ray Boone, stricken with cancer, made his way to Chicago's U.S. Cellular Field for the game. Two-time All-Star Ray joined four-time All-Star Bob, three-time All-Star Bret, and new All-Star Aaron for a photo on the field.

Two weeks later, the fifth-place, payroll-slashing Reds fired their manager, Bob Boone. Four days after that, Cincinnati completed de-Boone-ing the team by trading Aaron and his $3.7 million salary to the Yankees for a pair of pitching prospects, Brandon Claussen and Charlie Manning. Sitting in the clubhouse that day, Aaron wept. (The Boones get emotional.) Sportswriters pressed him to rip the Reds, but he wouldn't. "Hopefully," he said, "I can go to the Yankees, fit in, and be part of a winner."

It wasn't to be. At least not yet. Playing third

base beside Derek Jeter, the National League All-Star batted .254 with a paltry six homers in half a season in the Bronx. He hit so poorly in the playoffs that in Game Three of the 2003 American League Championship Series, Yankees manager Joe Torre started the light-hitting Enrique Wilson instead.

Aaron was as low as he'd ever been. Lacking his brother's pugnacity, the second third-generation Boone tended to brood. Rather than "Screw you," he thought, "What's wrong with me?"

Bret was in New York for the final game of the ALCS, serving as a color man for Fox TV. "It was kind of the ultimate show: Yankees and Red Sox at Yankee Stadium," he says. "Game Seven, with Pedro Martínez pitching for the Red Sox, Roger Clemens for the Yankees. The whole baseball world was buzzing. The Sox had won Game Six. One more and they might reverse the curse." That would be the Curse of the Bambino, dating back to 1918, the last time the Sox won the World Series. Now, eighty-five years and countless heartbreaks later, Boston would have its chance to hearse the curse—unless Aaron and the Yankees broke their hearts again.

"He was having a hell of a time, batting .125 in the series," Bret recalls. "I gave him a pep talk before the game. I said, 'Who knows, you might be oh-for-three, then you go up the last time and get the key hit.' And then he's not even *in* the game!"

Benched again, Aaron watched from the Yankees dugout as the Red Sox took a 4–2 lead into the eighth inning. Jason Giambi had kept New York close with a pair of solo homers, a minor miracle given Giambi's commute to the game. On his way to Yankee Stadium, he'd been caught in a miles-long snarl of traffic at the George Washington Bridge. A water main had burst, closing the bridge. Giambi was stuck—until police officers recognized the steroidal slugger waving his arms and gave him a lights-and-sirens escort to the ballpark.

In the bottom of the eighth, Sox manager Grady Little let a weary Pedro Martínez throw his 123rd pitch. New York tied the game. An inning later, Aaron Boone took over at third for Enrique Wilson. With the score tied at five, Aaron would face Boston knuckleballer Tim Wakefield in the eleventh inning.

Wakefield was about to become MVP of the Championship Series. He had won Games One and Four, allowing three runs in thirteen innings. He'd retired the Yankees in order in the bottom of the tenth, and he owned Aaron Boone, who had faced Wakefield five times in this ALCS and made five outs: three lazy fly balls and two strikeouts. But manager Torre had an idea. Torre had watched Boone get more anxious with every at-bat against the knuckleballer, triggering his swing an instant too soon, pulling balls foul. As

Aaron left the dugout to lead off the bottom of the eleventh, Torre said, "Try hitting him to right field. Maybe that'll help you keep it fair."

Wakefield finished his warm-ups. Aaron stepped to the plate, feeling his pulse in his ears. "Keep it simple," he thought. "It's just an AB. Right field, right field."

Bret, looking down from the broadcast booth, saw his brother dig his front foot into the reddish-brown clay of the batter's box. He thought, "Wakefield! A knuckleballer screws you up. On the other hand, Aaron's already screwed up. Maybe it'll work the other way, maybe a knuckler's what he needs to come out of it . . ."

Wakefield's first-pitch knuckler hung over the plate. Aaron promptly forgot all about right field. Torre's advice might have helped him keep his weight back an instant longer, but this ball wanted to be pulled. As it floated, muscle memory took over. Aaron planted his front foot, twisted his torso and drove the ball to left, while . . .

Bob Boone, watching on TV in a hunting lodge in Idaho, leaped out of his chair, and . . .

Bret stood up in the Fox broadcast booth, following the ball as it rose toward a clutch of delirious Yankees fans in the left-field seats who scrambled for the ball as Aaron began rounding the bases.

Cameras flashed all over the stadium. Aaron thrust both arms into the air. Loudspeakers rang with "New York, New York," which would play fourteen times in a row. Teammates mobbed the game's unlikely hero, who had an odd, sleepy thought in the midst of his career moment.

"I thought, 'What are all these people doing in my dream? I hope this is really happening.' "

"It was over so fast, that's what I remember," Wakefield recalls. "I'd been told I was going to be the series MVP if we won. Then it's over. One pitch. That's baseball."

Bret stood in the Fox broadcast booth, his eyes brimming with tears. His mic might as well have been dead. "The director was in my earphone, yelling, *'Bret, say something!'* But I couldn't. Aaron's rounding the bases, the crowd's going crazy, the whole team's waiting for him at the plate, and I'm just standing there, trying to get a handle on my feelings. Finally, the director goes, *'Bret, that's perfect. Letting the moment speak for itself!'* "

Giambi, Clemens, and David Wells were making their way to Monument Park beyond the left-field fence. Passing a bottle back and forth, they toasted Babe Ruth's plaque. "The Babe's shining on us," Wells said. "The curse lives!"

Bret pulled off his headphones and headed for the Yankees clubhouse. Not to cover the celebration, but to look for his brother. "Ordinarily, I'd never go into their locker room. The Yankees were the enemy. But I had to see him, so I snuck in." He found Aaron surrounded by celebrating teammates dousing him in champagne. The Boone brothers' eyes met. Neither could speak.

"He gave me one hell of a hug," Aaron recalls.

Says Bret, "That was such a cool, cool moment. There was nothing to say. A moment like that, you don't need to say 'I love you.'"

6

★ *Slumps and Rumors* ★
THE DAVISES

On April 19, 2010, two and a half hours after his flight from Buffalo landed at LaGuardia Airport, Ike Davis singled in his first big-league at-bat. That made Ike and his dad the 197th father-son combo in the major leagues' 143-year history. Four days later, the Mets' new first baseman clubbed his first big-league homer, a blast that landed on Shea Bridge at Citi Field, about 450 feet from home plate, more than halfway from the plate to Jac's Auto Body Shop on 126th Street. That evening, his father's phone chimed with a text message:

Got him, daddy-o

Since then, Ike has sent Ron the same post-game text after every home run.

Big leaguers get to select the walk-up music that plays them to the plate for home-game at-bats. Ike chose "Start Me Up," a Rolling Stones tune from his dad's Yankees days. His fast start featured two more homers and eight RBIs in his first week in the majors. After a few fans showed up wearing tarnished Eisenhower campaign buttons reading I LIKE IKE, the sixty-year-old buttons became a hot seller on eBay. The team brought out buttons of its own, along with I LIKE IKE pennants, coffee mugs, and T-shirts. "Five days after his major league debut, Ike Davis has become a folk hero," Mets columnist Howard Megdal wrote.

"I'm not a folk hero, just a rookie," Ike said. A hot-hitting rookie in the media capital of the world, he didn't seek the spotlight but didn't shrink from it, either. His outlook was as direct as his father's advice: see the ball, hit the ball, have a ball. By May, he was batting cleanup.

Ike's left-handed power reminded Mets fans of Darryl Strawberry. His hell-for-leather dives for foul balls drew ovations even on the road. Nimble for a big man, with the easy footwork around the bag that a first baseman needs, he was just as smooth fielding questions from New York's press corps. Asked about being Jewish, he said he was proud of his heritage but less than observant. Yes, he would play on Yom Kippur. Yes, he sometimes greeted clubhouse visitors with "Shalom." But no, he didn't see himself as a Jewish star in the Koufax mold. He thought it might be funny to say he couldn't be a "Jewish star" because he didn't have six sides. "But you don't want to be a wise-ass," he recalls. He did discuss his mother's worries that New York nightlife might offer too many distractions. (His parents had divorced in

1999, but everybody got along.) "My mom tells me to find a nice Jewish girl and settle down," he told reporters. A couple nights later, a female fan waved a sign at Citi Field: HEY IKE, I'M JEWISH & SINGLE.

He went on to bat .274 with 19 homers and 71 RBIs in 2010. Only Strawberry had ever hit more homers as a Mets rookie. Ike finished seventh behind Buster Posey in Rookie of the Year voting and was runner-up to the St. Louis Cardinals' Albert Pujols for the National League's Gold Glove award at first base. After watching a couple of his homers, the Braves' Chipper Jones, a six-time All-Star, said, "I don't think I've seen a guy, pound for pound, with more pop than he's got." How many hitters his age were better than Ike? Posey, probably. Andrew McCutchen and Mike Stanton (soon to be known as Giancarlo), maybe. But the list was short. Ike's future was so bright he needed eye black. And then he blinked. It was like the light had changed, a cloud crossing the sun, and everything looked different.

IN MAY OF HIS SOPHOMORE SEASON with the Mets, Ike Davis was batting .302 with seven home runs—a 31-homer pace—when the Rockies' Troy Tulowitzki skied a pop fly over the mound at Coors Field. Ike and third baseman David Wright collided. Wright made the catch, Ike rolled his ankle. The trainer said he might be out a week, but the injury lingered. Doctors at Manhattan's Hospital for Special Surgery diagnosed a sprain, then a bone bruise. He missed the rest of the season. The following spring, after spending the off-season at home in Scottsdale, he came down with valley fever, a fungal disease carried by spores endemic to the Arizona desert. When farming, storms, or construction projects disturb the soil, the spores rise into the air. If you breathe them, they can lodge in the lungs. A telltale rash on the legs often leads to weakness, fever, and aching joints. There is no known cure.

The fever sapped Ike's strength. Rather than going fishing after workouts, he slept all afternoon and woke feeling weaker. He gave up beer but felt hungover anyway. "You worry. Your family worries," he recalls. They knew about Diamondbacks first baseman Conor Jackson, who batted .300 in 2008, then contracted valley fever, and retired at the age of twenty-nine.

At Tradition Field, the Mets' spring-training headquarters, Ike made a muscle for reporters. He claimed he felt "strong as ever." It helped that his power came less from brute strength than from the long arms and thick wrists that snapped his 32-ounce bat through the strike zone. Unlike the weight-room sessions that betrayed his fatigue, that fast-twitch motion really did feel as good as ever. "Wait it out. Stay strong," he told himself. Meanwhile, Team Davis took action.

Ron's second wife, Kendall, heard about an immune-system booster called sea buckthorn. Dr. Oz recommended the stuff on TV, and it seemed to help. Ike perked up. Still, he slumped when the 2012 season began. By June, he was batting .158 with five home runs. He swore valley fever wasn't the problem. "I'll get going." Some Mets fans felt sorry for him. Others booed.

Ron kept telling him tomorrow would be a four-hit day. Ike couldn't help thinking that his dad, a pitcher, had never endured the grinding daily frustration of a batting slump. Facing major-league pitching six times a week can put anyone in a tailspin. You take the fat pitches and swing at the filthy ones. You try waiting for your pitch and the count's oh-and-two before you know it. Fooled again. The other team's starter always seems to be Kershaw, Hamels, or Strasberg. Before long, every waiter, cabdriver, and bartender in New York has a swing tip for you, and you try some of them, but there's no sure cure. A slump is like a fever. You wait it out and hope it's gone tomorrow.

His swing had always had its share of moving parts. He held his hands high, then dropped them as he rocked forward, setting his rhythmic stroke in motion with a weight shift that generated force through the torque of his core muscles. That swing was a rare combination of power and rhythm. When it worked, it created Ruthian home-run power. When it got off-kilter, he felt like he was waving a Nerf noodle at laser beams. Asked whether Ron had been giving him advice, he shrugged. "Your dad can't give you everything. It's like life. There's stuff you have to go through yourself."

During one of their talks, Ike mentioned how confused he was. How could hitting get so hard?

"You know that guy on the mound? He's getting paid, too," Ron said. "Give him a little credit. All you can do is have good ABs. Make a good swing and strike out, you can be proud of yourself. Like I'm proud of you."

"I'm getting booed."

"You call that booing? They're *still* booing me in Minnesota."

Finally Ike rediscovered his rhythm. From late June through the end of the season, he belted 27 home runs to finish with 32, fifth-best in the league. Despite a full-season batting average of .227, worst in the majors among first basemen who kept their jobs, he soon got a 600 percent raise. Thanks to his super-two status as an early-season call-up in 2010, he was eligible for arbitration in the 2012–13 off-season. The Mets offered $2.4 million, while Ike and his agent wanted $3,125,000. In a document titled *Ike Davis v. New York Metropolitans Baseball Club*, the Metropolitans stated their case. By its nature as a club's brief, urging the arbitrator to choose the lower figure, the twelve-page document was anti-Ike. It made for unpleasant reading.

"Davis had a disappointing season both at the plate and in the field," the Mets contended. They elaborated:

As a hitter, Davis produced a split of a .227 batting average (AVG), .308 on-base percentage (OBP), and a .462 slugging percentage (SLG). A closer look at Davis's numbers show even more disappointment. While his numbers after the All-Star break (.255/.346/.542) are a marked improvement to his pre All-Star break performance (.201/.271/.388), there is only an illusion of improvement . . . In fact, in four of the six months of the season Davis produced an AVG under .230, three months an OBP under .300, and three months of a SLG under .500. Davis posted these disappointing numbers while batting in the middle of the order with 462 of his 519 at-bats (ABs) coming in the four, five, or six spot in the lineup . . . Davis was tied for the third most errors of qualifying NL first-basemen with eight and had the third worst range factor of all qualifying MLB first-basemen, in front of Cincinnati's Joey Votto and Detroit's Prince Fielder, both far superior offensive players . . . In his first season in New York, Davis was a versatile contributor with 33 doubles, 19 home runs, a .351 on-base percentage, and three steals. Yet by his third season Davis morphed into a one-dimensional player . . . With Davis struggling while occupying such a prominent role in their lineup, it is no surprise that the Mets quickly faded from contention. The Mets remain hopeful that Davis can regain his pre-injury form and be their everyday first baseman of the future as the team aspires to reach the postseason, but after Davis's 2012 season these aspirations remain nothing more than wishful thinking.

Thinking back on his impending arbitration hearing, Ike lets out a long breath. "We stuck to our guns," he says. During a week of negotiations before the hearing, the Mets upped their offer to $3 million, then $3.12 million. The difference was now down to $5,000. Still, Team Davis said no. At the deadline, the Mets gave in.

Three point one-two-five million sounded almost abstract to Ike until he saw his next bank statement online. Ballplayers get paid every two weeks. His biweekly pre-tax pay in 2012 had been $19,488; now it was $120,192.

Kendall Davis's sea buckthorn seemed to work.

Reporting to spring training in March 2013, Ike pronounced himself free of valley fever, "ready to roll." His goal? "Not to suck."

Bleacher Report's Alan Horvath handicapped the coming season with a question: THE YEAR IKE DAVIS WINS HIS FIRST HOME RUN CROWN? "Davis stands alone as their one player with the special ability to stir fan imagination. The reason is as simple as it is raw: power," he wrote. "When Ike Davis hits a baseball, it stays hit." But when he missed, he kept missing. Another abysmal April spurred tabloid gossip; supposedly the Mets were concerned about the "nightlife habits" that had worried his mother two years before. What stung Ike was that the story was apparently leaked by the Mets. According to what the New York *Daily News* called "a baseball source," the team "will consider trading him in part because of concerns that he's resistant to coaching and stays out too late." Ike felt blind-sided. "I've never done anything wrong," he said. "I show up ready to play every day." He wondered aloud what "out too late" was supposed to mean. "When you leave the ballpark at 12, you go back to your place and it's 12:30. If you watch a movie, it's 2:30. Is that late? If I had a job where I had to wake up at six in the morning, it would be late, but I don't." Ike couldn't help wondering about his decision to play every day rather than pitch. What if he'd made the wrong choice?

His family suspected the team was looking for a scapegoat. The Mets had been going downhill under general manager Sandy Alderson. Ron Davis saw the rumors about Ike as an effort to shift the blame while asserting the club's power over players' lives. Back in Ron's day, major leaguers rolled into the clubhouse a couple hours before a game. On the road, the team bus left the hotel at 5 p.m. for a 7 o'clock game. But as meetings, stretching, weight training, and other pregame prep expanded, the job consumed more of the players' time. Now they arrived five or six hours before game time. The Mets held batting practice at 4:35 for 7:05 home games, but expected players to be at Citi Field for stretching exercises around 1 p.m. Management, media, and fans lauded "first to the ballpark, last to leave" workhorses like the Phillies' Chase Utley, as if having a life off the field were selfish. Ron links such practices to the game's injury epidemic. "It's overpreparation. All the stretching, lifting, and extra BP wears bodies out. Look at the trainers—they're bulked-up hulks. They could never play baseball without getting hurt."

After a game that typically lasted three hours, Ike would shower and grab a bite from the spread, the lavish postgame meal that evolved from hot dogs and cold cuts to tapas, prime rib, and sashimi as the game grew ever richer. Leaving the park around midnight after ten or eleven hours at work, he was inclined to unwind at a club, have a beer, smile for a few selfies with fans, maybe meet a nice Jewish girl. "I'm not a robot," he said. Nobody asked about the hours he kept when he was hitting, but he wasn't. Again. And the Mets kept hinting that he wasn't "coachable." At least he knew what they meant by that. They meant he wanted to stick with the hitting style that got him to the majors in the first place.

General manager Alderson had come to New York from Oakland, where he had mentored Billy Beane. Along with stats guru Paul DePodesta, they hatched the *Moneyball* approach, based on selective hitting and on-base percentage, that was immortalized in Michael Lewis's book and in the movie in which Brad Pitt played Beane. When Alderson, a lean ex-Marine who earned his law degree at Harvard, moved on to New York, DePodesta joined him as the Mets' farm-system director. This was the last thing the rest of the National League wanted to see. Unlike small-market Oakland, the Mets were a wealthy franchise. They could play "moneyball with money," a potentially dominant model in which Beane's old allies outbid him for players. The Mets promptly launched a version of the Oakland plan they dubbed "hunting strikes," in which Mets minor leaguers were told to work every count. Free swinging was for losers. At first, the most selective minor leaguers might get a pat on the butt and a positive note in the manager's nightly report to the parent club; starting in 2012, they got rewards they could spend. Under a scheme called BPO (bases per out), Mets farm-hands got a $200 bonus for each "base earned" and were docked $100 for each out they made.

Soon the team brought the system to the major-league level. Knowing that $200 wouldn't get major leaguers' attention, club officials raised the stakes with a new metric that gave batters a plus for each pitch they took that was called a ball and each strike they swung at, and a minus for taking a strike or swinging at a pitch outside the zone. Rather than offering bonuses or fines, coaches and executives suggested that hitters' pluses and minuses could affect future contract offers, and perhaps playing time.

Manager Terry Collins and hitting coach Dave Hudgens were tasked with selling the plan to the players. Wright, an All-Star third baseman and team captain, was exempt. He could do as he pleased. So could Curtis Granderson, the $60 million outfielder Alderson had signed before the season began. Everyone else was expected to hunt strikes. Ike was all ears until he heard that results didn't matter in the Mets' strike hunt: if you swung at a pitch half an inch inside and hit a grand slam, you got a minus.

In Scottsdale, watching his son check his swing on the MLB Network, Ron said that "hunting strikes" reminded him of the Angels' pitching philosophy in the 1990s. The Angels had offered him a scouting job with a caveat: don't bother to send a report on any pitchers under six foot two. Ron laughed when he heard that. So much for Ron Guidry, Pedro Martínez, Greg Maddux, Billy Wagner, and a hundred others. "They take a general rule and make a religion out of it," he said now. "So what if it's stupid? If the team wins, they're heroes. If not, they get fired and go run another team."

Despite his doubts, Ike bought in. Working with hitting coach Hudgens, a man with a perpetually gloomy hound-dog expression, he shortened his stride, spreading his stance until he was practically doing the splits. He lowered his hands, raised them, loosened his grip on the bat. "I tried everything," he says. When nothing worked, Hudgens said what coaches say when they're out of ideas.

"You're thinking too much. Let it *flow*."

Ike tried to let it flow. It didn't. When Hudgens asked him to open or close his stance, he tried that. When he struck out and Hudgens said, "You're better than that," Ike refrained from saying, "I was before you started screwing with my swing."

His defense suffered. Later, he admitted to taking his offensive woes out to first base with him. By now, the *New York Times* was calling him

"No-Hit, No-Field Davis." At one point, tying himself in mental and physical knots, he had two hits in 44 at-bats. In June 2013, the Mets sent him to the minors. "First and foremost, Ike needs to clear his head," said Alderson.

"I'm going to go down, work hard, and figure out my swing," Ike said.

"He's made so many changes. Too many," said Triple-A manager Wally Backman, one of a few straight talkers in the organization. "We'll try to get him back to what he did to get to the big leagues. Mentally, he's totally fucked up."

After three and half years of major-league Westins and Hyatt Regencys, Ike never expected to see the El Paso Holiday Inn again, or to pick at a Pacific Coast League spread of sandwiches and wilted salads. With Backman barking encouragement, he went back to his natural stance. He hit his way back to New York in two weeks, batting .364 for Backman's Las Vegas 51s. Rejoining the Mets in July, determined to prove he belonged, he stuck to his old stance but cut down his swing. "You can drop the bat on the ball for a single over the infield," he reminded himself. "You can pull a grounder down the line." From July through mid-September, when a rib injury ended his season, he batted .286 with an on-base percentage of .449. Not surprisingly, his power numbers dropped. He hit only four homers in the second half. Still, Ike Davis, the guy the Mets thought couldn't hunt strikes, was suddenly reaching base almost half the time. His second-half on-base percentage was the club's highest by far. It was better than the full-season OBP of Detroit's Miguel Cabrera, who won the American League's Triple Crown. Yet the Mets brass had their doubts. In baseball, there are few things more suspect than tweeners. Was their twenty-six-year-old first baseman fish or fowl? A home-run hitter or a slap hitter? Was he a head case?

According to Peter Gammons, "The curious part of Ike Davis is that if you piece together elements of his seasons, you have an elite player. The 2010 Ike Davis was an elite defender making highlight-reel catches. The 2012 Ike Davis was a power threat, a 30-home-run guy capable of driving in a hundred men. Ike Davis 2013, or the little we saw of him, was a walk machine." But as Gammons told his ESPN audience, "If all of Ike's strengths came together, he could be an All-Star. But if he continues struggling to put things together, he could find himself out of a starting job."

IKE KEPT AN APARTMENT IN SCOTTSDALE along with his bachelor pad in New York. He couldn't get much more than moral support from his family during the season, but in the off-season of 2013–14, he relied on a batting-practice pitcher with pinpoint control and an old-time attitude.

Four times a week, he rolled out of bed and drove twenty minutes to a sun-scraped diamond in Cholla Park, where Ron and his Sidewinders practiced.

They began by pulling Ron's L-screen from the back of his truck and dragging it to the mound. A chain-link shield in the shape of the letter *L*, the seven-foot screen allowed a hurler to throw batting practice without getting beaned by line drives. Ron never threw BP without it, not even to thirteen-year-olds who sent liners up the middle at 70 or 80 miles an hour. Liners off Ike's wooden bat struck the screen at speeds up to 120, sometimes lifting it off the ground.

Ike stepped to the plate at Cholla Park with his hands high and his feet shoulder-width apart, the stance that got him to the majors. Ron fed him straightballs in and out, up and down.

"Everybody's shifting on you," he said. Major-league defenses now shifted on more and more batters, left-handed pull hitters in particular, moving the shortstop to the second-base side of the field and leaving the third baseman alone on the left side. Driven by data on hitters' tendencies—data showing where every player hit every sort of pitch in every situation—the shifts evolved from a Tampa Bay Rays specialty to a game-wide trend that brought run production to thirty-year lows. In 2011, major-league defenses greeted batters with a shift about 2,500 times. Three years later, the number topped 14,000. Ron thought his son could boost his batting average with hits to the opposite field. "You shorten up, let the ball get a little deeper," he said, flipping a high-seventies fastball across the outside corner.

"I know." Ike drew his hands closer to his chest. He waited a split-second, then slapped a grounder past third base. The ball skipped in the bone-dry outfield, kicking up dirt.

"Ha!" Ron said. "It's Rod Carew. Tony Gwynn—"

"Ike Davis," Ike said, touching the bill of his cap.

Some of the Sidewinders showed up early when Ike was in town. They hooted and whistled at the moon shots he launched past the outfield light towers 360 feet away, toward Frank Lloyd Wright Boulevard and the McDowell Mountains in the distance. When Ike hit one hard, the impact made a sharp *crack,* the sound of big-league contact. If you stood near first base, you could hear his line drives go by, audibly sizzling through the air.

After batting practice, he threw a football around with the kids, sending them on fly patterns to the outfield, hitting them with sixty-yard strikes. Ron watched for a while before raising his hands. "Fun's over!" He told them to quit playing football before they got concussions.

While Ike wintered in Arizona, the Mets discussed trading him. The Brewers and Pirates were looking for a first baseman. The Orioles offered pitcher Zach Britton, but the Mets said no. The team's owners, Fred Wilpon and Saul Katz, had lost an estimated $500 million in Bernie Madoff's notorious Ponzi scheme. Now they were said to be losing $70 million a year as "moneyball with money" turned into what the *Post* dubbed an "Amazin' Mess." Hunting strikes wasn't helping. The Mets scored fewer runs every year from 2011 to 2014. Even by their own lights, Alderson and DePodesta seemed to be missing a key difference between moneyball in Oakland and Metsball in New York. In Oakland, working with Beane, they drafted and traded for players who fit their approach. In New York, they imposed their approach on players they already had, hitters as different as Ike, Wright, and slap-hitting base stealer Eric Young Jr.

While he was discussing Ike with other GMs, Alderson signed free-agent outfielder Chris Young for $7.25 million, a move that meant incumbent left fielder Lucas Duda would now be a first baseman. "I still like Ike," manager Collins announced. Alderson preferred Duda, who was more selective at the plate.

In December 2013, David Wright married his longtime girlfriend, Molly Beers, in Los Gatos, California. At the reception, Alderson pulled Ike aside and asked if he believed in what the Mets were doing. Could the team count on him? "Absolutely," Ike said.

"We are not going to move Ike just to move Ike," Alderson announced a month later. Baseball's hot-stove season, he said, "is a trade market, not a yard sale, and we're perfectly happy to go into the season with both Davis and Duda."

Batting sixth on Opening Day, Ike went oh-for-two with a walk. Duda and right-handed-hitting Josh Satin started the next two games, making the 2014 Mets the first major-league team ever to start a different first baseman in the first three games of a season. Collins and Alderson pronounced themselves pleased with this arrangement. They would play the hot hand, play matchups with opposing pitchers, or rotate first basemen, if not consult Abbott and Costello. A day later, Collins announced a new policy: Duda, who was oh-for-six so far in the new season, would be the primary first baseman. "He's earned it," the manager said.

Ike accepted the club's choice. He and Duda were friends. "I hope he hits," he said. "It's not his fault we're going for the same ABs."

"The Mets screwed up," Ron told the *Daily News*. "They told my son, 'We don't want you anymore.' They got close to trading him over the winter but they messed that up, and it was,

'Well, heck, we may have to keep him.' I told Ike, 'You're like a piece of hamburger meat at the grocery store. When you're first put out there in that wrapper you look real good, bright and red. And the older you get, you get a little brownish, and people don't want to pick you up." In one sense, this was just Ron popping off. In another, it amounted to a tactic: Ron hoped that publicly disparaging the Mets might deflect some of the pressure from his son to him, the disgruntled dad, while getting Ike's side of the story out. Maybe it would spur Alderson to trade Ike to a team that would play him. And maybe it served as therapy, too. Ron told no one but his wife how he ached over Ike's benching. He certainly didn't tell Ike.

On April 5, the day after the Mets named Duda their first-string first baseman, they trailed Cincinnati 3–2 in the bottom of the ninth inning. After New York loaded the bases, Collins sent Ike to pinch-hit. Ike took a strike, then timed a J. J. Hoover curve and lined it off the facade of the second deck. It was the Mets' first walk-off grand slam since 1991. A minute later, while teammates mobbed him and pitcher Jonathon Niese delivered a shaving-cream pie to the hero's face, Collins called the victory "a tremendous ending for Ike, going through what he's going through."

LATER IN APRIL, Ron let his 24–0 Sidewinders go home early. The Mets were in town. He stowed his ball bucket and L-screen in his Tahoe and jockeyed through rush-hour traffic to Chase Field, home of the Diamondbacks.

"The Mets are the team they are because of indecision," he said, spitting tobacco into a paper cup. "Are they contenders or rebuilders? Do they want to trade Isaac, or don't they? They're damned either way. They're scared to death he'll come back and haunt them." He said he hated seeing baseball get more corporate every year, becoming a numbers-driven business that sought to turn men into products defined solely by their stats. He'd laughed when he heard a TV executive describe ballgames as content. "There's some very smart men running ball clubs, Harvard men and Stanford men, but there's different ways of being smart, just like there's different ways to pitch or hit. Playing taught me that. Being a coach and a father taught me that, because every kid's different. The Mets' general manager, he's a Harvard man, but did he ever put on a jockstrap and play?" As for manager Collins, a former minor-league teammate of Ron's who never reached Double-A ball, Ron was his usual plainspoken self. "He's a puppet. He's just trying to keep his job. The general manager fills out the lineup card for him."

Chase Field in downtown Phoenix resembles a mall. There's a Cold Stone Creamery, a Panda Express, and a Subway sandwich shop in the mezzanine. The place is clean and comfortable but devoid of the peanuts-and-Cracker-Jack-and-beer tang of Wrigley, Fenway, or the old Yankee Stadium. One part of Chase Field smells like chlorine—the swimming pool beyond the right-field fence, where home-run balls splash between frolicking fans.

Ron lumbered upstairs to join a dozen friends and family members in a mezzanine suite stocked with beer and wine, soft drinks, peanuts, nachos, and inch-thick chocolate chip cookies.

By then, Ike had been at the park for more than five hours. He wasn't in the lineup that night; Duda was starting. Ike's name was among those of the other substitutes clumped below the starters' names on the lineup card posted in the dugout. That meant he took batting practice with the substitutes. He smoked several balls into the seats, including one that cleared the swimming pool beyond the right-field fence, before trudging through the dugout to the clubhouse.

"First, you get hydrated," he said later, describing his pregame routine. "Stretch, then hot tub. Work out. Then it's meetings." Hitters meet with the batting coach to go over scouting reports on the other team's pitchers. "Then it's video—watching the other guys' starting pitcher. If I'm not in the lineup, I'll take a look at him but focus more on relievers." While Wright, Granderson, Duda, and the other starters watched clips of

Bronson Arroyo, Ike studied Arizona setup man Brad Ziegler and closer Addison Reed to prep for a possible pinch-hit at-bat. "After that, you stretch with the team, hit BP, take grounders. Get a snack in the clubhouse. Take a shower before the game. Restretch. Then the game starts."

Two levels up, Ron sat with Kendall, a striking redhead, and Ike's sister Tracy. The three of them wore gold wedding bands matching the one on Ike's throwing hand. When Ron and Kendall married in 1999, "We melded families," Ron explained. "She had two kids from her previous marriage and I had my three. We gave them all wedding rings, and all seven of us walked down the aisle. We are *fam-a-lee*."

When the Mets took the field, Duda trotted out to first base. Ike stayed in the dugout. He was learning that a big-league bench can be a lonely place. With nine men on the field and five or six relievers in the bullpen, only ten or eleven players remained—four starting pitchers who wouldn't be used that night, plus six or seven substitutes—in a dugout that seated thirty.

The Diamondbacks shifted on Duda in the bottom of the first, posting third baseman Martín Prado at the shortstop position, all by himself on the left side. Ike had foiled shifts twice in the season's early going, slapping a single and a double to left. Tonight, Duda grounded out to first to drive in a run.

Upstairs, Ron was getting antsy. When a friend asked how Ike was handling his benching, Ron craned his neck, trying to see into the Mets dugout. "It's hard on him," he said. "It's hard on all of us. Hell, it's hard on Duda." He paced the suite. "They talk like he's a flop, but his first year was a good one. The next year he's leading the team in homers, average, and RBIs when he hurts his leg. Then he had a bad year, but show me a major leaguer who hasn't had a bad year." He sounded like a million dads making excuses for their kids. Still, he was right on all counts, including a follow-up. "What you better not do at his age," he said, "is have two bad years in a row."

Two innings later, Duda grounded out again. Ike stayed loose by riding a stationary bike in the clubhouse, watching the game on TV. What was he thinking? "You tell yourself to stay in the game," he said later. "See how they're pitching our lefties. Stay loose. I want to be ready when I get up there." He corrected himself: "If."

As Art Cook liked to say, "They also serve who only pinch-hit."

The Mets chased Arroyo with a six-run fourth. Ike applauded. Ron fretted that a big lead could keep Ike from getting a pinch-hit at-bat. On the other hand, he didn't want his son going up in the ninth inning of a blowout. That's a guillotine AB, one that's likely to get cut short. A reliever with a big lead can nibble. The strike zone grow may grow as the plate umpire pictures his dinner. Good luck hunting strikes when your neck's on that chopping block.

The game ended with Ike on the dugout's top step, still waiting his turn.

THREE DAYS LATER, Ike was dressing for a game against the Atlanta Braves when Collins called him into the manager's office.

In Scottsdale, Ron took a call from his son's agent. "There's something cooking," Nero said. Ron switched on the TV and watched the ESPN ticker at the bottom of the screen. The ticker crept through NBA scores and WNBA news on its way to the letters he was looking for: MLB. Nothing. He watched another cycle of sports news, back around to MLB, and there it was: NEW YORK METS TRADE IKE DAVIS . . .

He was out of his chair as their surname crossed the screen. Punching the air, calling to his wife, "Here's what he needs!"

Minor-league all-star Art Cook won 21 games for the
Border League's Kingston Ponies in 1948.

"Lefty" Cook's teammates gave him the hero treatment
after a victory in Indianapolis.

Thirteen-year-old Ike Davis played for Ron Davis's youth-league team in Scottsdale, Arizona, in 1990. (COURTESY OF THE DAVIS FAMILY)

Ike Davis (left) met his dad, Ron, outside the Mets' locker room at Citi Field in 2010, Ike's rookie year. (COURTESY OF THE DAVIS FAMILY)

Traded to the Pirates in 2014, benched against left-handed pitchers, Ike Davis faced an uncertain future. (CHARLES LECLAIRE/USA TODAY SPORTS)

Dan Haren Sr. pushed Dan Jr., a Little League star, so hard that the boy "hated it." But it worked. (COURTESY OF DAN HAREN SR.)

During the Dodgers' race for the 2014 pennant, thirty-four-year-old Dan Haren found himself pitching for his career. (JAYNE KAMIN-ONCEA/USA TODAY SPORTS)

From a cushioned diamond to the rules—three strikes and you're still up—Miracle League Baseball levels the field for disabled kids. (COURTESY OF MIRACLE LEAGUE BASEBALL)

Four All-Stars named Boone (left to right: Bob, Bret, Ray, and Aaron) at Philadelphia's Veterans Stadium in the mid-1970s. (COURTESY OF THE BOONE FAMILY)

Retired from the majors since 2009, Aaron Boone now broadcasts baseball for ESPN. (COURTESY OF ESPN IMAGES)

Bret Boone (left) followed son Jake's progress with the Bears, an elite southern California travel team. (COURTESY OF BRET BOONE)

Bret and Jake on their way to a game. (COURTESY OF BRET BOONE)

Art Cook threw a sneaky fastball, a curve, and a screwball that kept right-handed hitters off balance.

Dusty Baker (left) with son Darren. At age three, Darren was almost run over at the plate during the 2002 World Series. (FRANK VICTORES/USA TODAY SPORTS)

Julia Ruth with "Daddy" near the Yanks' spring training complex in St. Petersburg, Florida, in the 1930s. (COURTESY OF JULIA RUTH STEVENS AND TOM STEVENS)

As she neared her 100th birthday, Julia threw ceremonial first pitches "to keep Daddy's memory alive." (MARK J. REBILAS/USA TODAY SPORTS)

First-base coach Bobby Bonds teamed up with son
Barry in their season with the Giants in 1996. (PHIL
CARTER/USA TODAY SPORTS)

TOMORROW NIGHT

IS

ART COOK
Appreciation
Night

AT MEGAFFIN MEMORIAL STADIUM

Making his first local appearance
of the season.

See the DOUBLEHEADER

Auburn Cayugas vs. Ponies

FIRST GAME STARTS AT 7 O'CLOCK
Tickets Obtainable at Pony Sport Shop and Rikely and Vince

ADMISSION: GRANDSTAND, 90c—BLEACHERS, 60c

In 1949, fans filled Megaffin Stadium to salute
"the Border League's greatest lefthander."

Cal Cook (right)
joined the author
for a pilgrimage to
the park in
Kingston, Ontario,
where Art "Lefty"
Cook once pitched.
(COURTESY OF
DOUG GRAHAM)

7

★ Looking for the Cure ★
ART COOK, MIDLIFE

The Border League's doubleheader-winning "Iron Man" spent three seasons pitching through what the *Kingston Whig-Standard* termed his "arm miseries." By 1954, his fastball was gone. He bounced from the Class C Ogdensburg Maples to the Class D Union City Greyhounds to the Kitchener Panthers of Ontario's semipro Intercounty League, where "Lefty" Cook faced ex-prospects and beer-bellied locals. His shoulder ached. His elbow barked every time he tried to snap a screwball. There was no talk of rotator cuffs or ulnar collateral ligaments in those days, just sore arms. Sore arms went home.

After throwing his last professional pitch in Kitchener, twenty-nine-year-old Art drove three hours to Windsor, Ontario, and crossed the Ambassador Bridge to Detroit. From there it was 280 miles through Michigan and Ohio to central Indiana and the rest of his life.

He made it back to Moral Township in time for the 1954 basketball season. "Art was the type of coach whose players swear he's too hard on them," said his coaching rival Leroy Compton. "Then they graduate and love him the rest of their life." Coach Cook led Moral to four Shelby County basketball titles between 1951 and 1956, the first four county crowns in school history. And just before the '56 season, he became a father. An early photo shows Arthur and Patricia Cook's first child—me, a ten-month-old in a diaper and a miniature Moral Hawks jersey—preparing to dunk a mini-basketball in a wastebasket.

In 1959, Dad moved from tiny Moral Township to his old high school, Franklin Central, just south of Indianapolis, where he turned an 11–10 team into a 22–4 conference champion. A year later, his Franklin Flashes won a second straight conference title. Coach Cook was a minor celebrity, giving newspaper and radio interviews while his little boy crawled up and down the bleachers in the gym. Sometimes I'd be in the top row, stretching my chubby fingers toward the scoreboard, when the scoreboard horn went off. At arm's length, the sound was deafening. All you can do if you're four when that happens is grab a bleacher seat, hold on, and try not to pee.

We lived on the city's suburban east side, twenty minutes from the school. Our gray ranch house sat on an acre of lawn that Dad and I mowed together. We'd play hand-over-hand with a bat to see who got to ride his pride-and-joy John Deere. Loser had to trim along the neighbors' fences with a gas-powered push mower and use a Weed Eater for close work around the backstop. Dad and his friends had pooled their efforts and labor to build a backyard diamond complete with a mound, pitcher's rubber, and chalk foul lines. The diamond didn't stay private for long. Kids came from all directions to play on it. Some summer days we played nine-on-nine, nine-inning games, taking time-outs for races up the driveway to Franklin Road when we heard the siren song of a Mr. Softee truck. If a neighbor kid had no money for a curly-top cone, Dad paid. Our house, about two hundred feet from the plate in right field, was in play. The rubber-coated hardballs we used left dents in the rain gutters and the aluminum door to the back porch. Dad usually pitched for one team while I pitched for the other. His buddy Norman Hartman, a tall, nearsighted fellow, stood behind the backstop calling balls and stee-rikes. Norman came from Martinsville, where he'd followed John Wooden onto the high school basketball squad and another local athlete, John Dillinger, on the town's sandlots. He liked to tell us how young Johnny Dillinger, jackrabbit shortstop for the semipro Martinsville Athletics, staged his first holdup with help from a local umpire. They were robbing a grocery when Dillinger shot the grocer. The ump lost his nerve and took off in the getaway car. Dillinger got caught and wound up playing short for the prison team at the Indiana State Reformatory.

Norman idolized Dad. Both men missed the action of their playing days. Norman's playing career had ended at Butler, where they were basketball teammates, while Dad's extended through college, amateur baseball, and the minor leagues. Now they "kept a hand in," as they said, with occasional bets on ballgames. Sometimes they bet with a bookie. Norman, who never married, would end up in Las Vegas, gambling on sports every day, but in those days he spent his summer afternoons at our house. He and Dad listened to Reds and Cubs games, pored over betting lines and pitching matchups, and needled each other in the way aging athletes do.

"Bunt," Norman would advise me in a loud voice when I batted against Dad. "Your old man can't get off the mound like he used to." But I wasn't looking for singles. It was 300 feet down the left-field line to the Schifferdeckers' fence and 200 to the house in right, but only 160 to straightaway center, where our driveway cut into the outfield. Dad used to park his car halfway up the driveway, out of reach of all but the longest shots, and offer five dollars to anyone who hit a homer off his car. I spent two or three summers trying to win that fiver, but he wouldn't allow it. He'd groove slowballs to other boys and to Cathy Lenahan, the tomboy Dad thought I should marry someday so he could have big-league grandsons, but he pitched me tougher, pinning the ball to my hands or fading it over the outside corner. "Just pitching to the park," he said.

One day, I drove one of his pitches to right. My grandmother was making sandwiches for us, spreading Jif and Welch's grape jelly on Wonder bread, when the ball flew through the window seven or eight feet away, sending glass all over the place. Nana jumped, but kept her Hoosier composure. This had happened before. She *tsk-tsk*ed and lobbed the ball back out the window.

Dad made me clean up the glass. But he was smiling. "You got that one pretty good. Maybe I should pitch you harder," he said.

AT BAT, he punched grounders or looping fly balls for me and the neighborhood kids to chase. If the other team needed an out, Norman the ump called him out on strikes, sometimes on balls that bounced on the plate or went over his head. They both thought that was funny. Only occasionally would Dad show us what he could still do. He'd make a show of digging in at the plate, aiming his bat at the house. On the next hittable pitch, he'd shift his weight at the last instant, his left wrist turning over his right, delivering the bat's barrel to the ball with a *clack* that was the ball's way of saying goodbye. "Arthur, you've still got it," Norman would say. "He's still got it, boys and girls!" We'd watch the ball sail over the chimney. Then we'd hurry around the house to find it in the front yard, or in a ditch on the far side of Franklin Road. One day, I walked off the distance. It was 390 feet from the backstop to the ditch.

When his friends dropped by—an old team-mate, another high school coach or assistant, an ex-jock neighbor—they liked to challenge him. "Let's see the good stuff. I bet I could hit you." Every now and then he gave in to temptation. My friends and I loved this routine: Dad began by turning to the kids playing defense behind him. "Sit down, take it easy," he said. "This won't take long." It was a bit he'd picked up from Eddie Feigner, a fast-pitch softballer who used to barn-storm through the minors with a four-man team known as The King and His Court. Like the Harlem Globetrotters, they were showmen with talent. The crew-cut Feigner's underhand fastball was clocked at 104 miles an hour. He could throw 90 behind his back or between his legs. With a Court consisting only of a catcher, first baseman, and shortstop, he beat all-star teams for fifty years, pitching 238 perfect games—you can look it up. In a 1967 exhibition, Feigner struck out Willie Mays, Willie McCovey, Brooks Robinson, Roberto Clemente, Maury Wills, and Harmon Killebrew: six up, six down. Sometimes he'd give his fielders a theatrical wave. "Relax! Take it easy." They would sit or lie down while Feigner struck out the side.

Dad gave his buddies the Feigner treatment. Some were ten or fifteen years younger than he was, former college jocks just starting their coaching careers. One, Fred Jones, had been a college football star. Like the rest, Jones swung and missed. And looked surprised. Dad didn't throw as hard as he used to, but our mound was closer to the plate—the Little League distance of forty-six feet rather than sixty feet, six inches— and the difference between the lollipops he tossed us kids and the 80-ish zip he kept in reserve made his fastball look quicker. He'd turn his back to the plate during his windup, like Luis Tiant, hiding the ball so that it seemed to come out of nowhere. Some of his victims couldn't react. They stood there without swinging. Some waved at the ball after it went by. Others tried to time him. Twitching with eagerness, they'd start swinging as he released the ball. That's when Dad pulled the string, floating a changeup that crossed the plate after they swung.

A few of them fouled one off or bounced a grounder somewhere, but the vast majority struck out. Some cussed. The other kids and I mimicked them—"Shit! Fuckit!" The grown-ups I liked were the ones who took their medicine the right way. Larry, a former high school hoops All-American who went on to the Indiana Basketball Hall of Fame, waved at three pitches without so much as a foul tip. He dropped his bat and bowed toward the mound, slowly clapping his hands. Dad bowed back.

I was twelve or thirteen when I told Dad, "Give me your best."

He said, "Really?"

"Really."

He stepped behind the mound to make it fairer. From there, about fifty-five feet from the plate, he flipped a straight fastball about 60 miles an hour. I let it go. "Your *best,*" I said. He shrugged. He wound up and threw me a screwball. Not his best one, not with twenty years of rust on his arm, but I can still not see it now. As I started my swing, the ball was center-cut, right down the middle. Then it disappeared, diving off the outside corner. I missed it by a foot.

"Strike!" Norman said.

Dad grooved the next one, a gift that I knocked over the driveway fence. With those two pitches, he delivered two messages. The first had to do with the levels of the game. As he liked to say, the distance from backyard baseball—or even college ball—to the lowest levels of pro ball was a "mink stole": a fur piece. His second pitch said, "You're my boy and I love you. Hit me."

During basketball season, Coach Cook held court in a diner where old men rehashed the Hoosier high school games of Oscar Robertson and Bobby Plump. Dad humored the old-timers by asking them whether his Franklin Central Flashes should play man-to-man, a zone, or a box-and-one. His teams of farm boys won conference and county titles but lost to Indianapolis schools in the state tournament. His best friend, Jim Rosenstihl, coached the legendary jump shooter Rick Mount at Lebanon High School. Mount was the first high school athlete to make the cover of *Sports Illustrated*. Rosenstihl brought him around to our house, where I rebounded for Mount, standing under the net while he drilled jumpers from all over the driveway. As good as Mount was, Dad held his own in their driveway shooting contests, lofting his old-fashioned set shot.

At thirteen, I was a Little League all-star. I didn't throw very hard, but I threw strikes. A Little League coach gave me a page showing my stats for the 1969 season: eight wins, no losses, an earned run average of 0.20. He said, "You'll mow 'em down in Pony League next year."

Pony League hitters disagreed. At thirteen and fourteen, the age of Ron Davis's Scottsdale Sidewinders, they were bigger and stronger than Little Leaguers. They turned my straightballs into doubles and long home runs like the one Dad had hit off me in the father-son game the year before. The mound was no place for a one-trick Pony Leaguer, a control artist without an out pitch, and as hard as he tried, Dad couldn't help me spin the ball enough to make it curve. After one frustrating session in the backyard, he said I was just one step from unhittable. Having mastered the hanging curve, all I had to do was get the hanging out of it.

As a freshman in high school, I played for the JV team, pinch-hitting and warming a spot on the bench. Sometimes I scanned the aluminum bleachers to see if Dad was there. He wasn't. I had one highlight that season: a pinch-hit appearance late with the score tied. With two out in the ninth, my chubby, bespectacled self singled to center to win the game. It wasn't the Shot Heard 'Round the World, or even 'round the block, but I couldn't wait to get home and tell Dad. "I pinch-hit in the ninth—"

"Fastball," he said. "First pitch, a shot up the middle."

"You saw it?" He'd been watching from his car in the parking lot. He didn't want me to know, didn't want to put pressure on me. "How many games have you been at?"

"A couple," he said. We went out for pizza that night, Dad's treat. For the star of the game, he said.

We shared the sport in other ways. He and I never sat around discussing anything, but we could always talk baseball for a minute or two. Some of my earliest memories are of him checking in on me at bedtime. I was five or six years old, still scared of monsters in the closet. He'd come in to say goodnight. He'd sit on the edge of the bed and ask, "What's the score?" He knew I had a transistor radio under my pillow, to listen to the Reds game while I fell asleep. He knew the score, too; I was pretty sure he'd been listening to the game in the other room. Asking was his way of saying goodnight. Maybe even, "Goodnight, I love you." My saying "Three-two Reds in the fifth" or something like that was a way to say the same.

Every April, he let me stay home from school to watch the Reds' Opening Day. The same went for the World Series. Not the whole Series, but I could stay home to see the first game and the seventh if there was a seventh game. My mother, to her credit, agreed with our idea of secular holidays.

Dad took me to meet a bleary-eyed Mickey Mantle at the opening of a men's clothing store— I've still got the Mick's autograph—and in the spring of 1969 we drove to Cincinnati, where Dad gave me a copy of *The Pete Rose Story* signed "To Kevin" by Charlie Hustle himself, my headfirst-sliding hero. I was still whooping about that when we pulled up beside the still-under-construction Riverfront Stadium. The vast, unlined parking lot was empty except for a couple of forklifts. A sleepy-looking security guard sat in a folding chair at the only unlocked entrance. Dad chatted him up; a bill changed hands. A couple minutes later, we were alone on the field, looking up at row after row of blue and green and red seats. I ran my hand over the infield grass—the first time I felt the toothbrush texture of Astroturf. "Run the bases," Dad said.

A future crowd of fifty thousand cheered as I chugged around the bases and slid headfirst into home. From that day on, he said I was the one who scored the first run at Riverfront.

One night, we were sitting by the Philco TV in the family room, Dad with his White Owl cigar and ashtray, me with my algebra homework. He fiddled with the TV's rabbit-ear antenna, bending it toward the window. The picture faded and sharpened as Reds reliever Billy McCool walked a batter.

"Billy Goddamn McCool." Dad reached for his *Gold Sheet*, the glossy "Bettor's Bible" he picked up every week at a downtown newsstand. He crossed out the bets he'd lost that day, put check marks by the winners. He had a bet on the Reds, who looked like a lock with one out in the ninth and hard-throwing McCool on the mound. Two walks and an infield single later, the bases were loaded and it was clear that no one in human history had stunk more than McCool, who proceeded to give up a game-losing liner up the middle as Dad tossed the *Gold Sheet*—just as shortstop Leo Cárdenas snagged the ball and doubled the runner off second. Dad wins!

Our celebration brought my mother to the family room. She saw how happy we were, yelling and jumping around, and knew why. A bet. She shut the door.

• • •

IN THE EARLY '70S, Dad launched a small-time bookmaking business, mostly as a favor to his friends. There was Denny, a former hoops star who was now an assistant coach, and Steve, another local coach. Fred, the former college cornerback. Buddy, Jeff, a couple guys named John. Dad booked their bets for two reasons. The first was to keep the action close to home. Why should he and his cronies rely on a bookie? Dad had the *Gold Sheet* to set the lines (which he tweaked to take advantage of Buddy's weakness for the Reds or Steve's habit of betting on the Cardinals). His second incentive was the vig. Short for vigorish, an old Russian word borrowed from the loan-sharking world, the vig is a book-maker's cut of the action. It usually works out to 4½ to 5 percent, but can reach 10 percent, making sports betting a game in which you actually have to give 110 percent. On a good day, the vig might pay for our spaghetti and meatballs at Dad's favorite restaurant, Italian Gardens, with candles and wicker-clad Chianti bottles on the tables. The vig also kept his asthmatic sedans topped up with gas. He practically collected old cars. He would write off all or part of a buddy's gambling debt in exchange for an old heap and drive it till it boiled over once too often. At that point, he'd get it going one last time and putter to Indianapolis Raceway Park, where he would trade the car to a demolition derby promoter for a fifty-dollar bill. I tagged along a couple times. I liked the dust and noise and gear-churning chaos of cars ramming hoods on a figure-eight track until only one was left to take a muddy, flat-tired victory lap among the losers' steaming husks. We'd get a lift home from one of the demo drivers, sweaty men who tended to look like Johnny Cash or Jerry Lee Lewis and smelled so strongly of gas and motor oil that I thought they might catch fire when they lit their cigarettes.

If Dad was booking that night, he'd want to get home before the West Coast games started. He'd need to be by the phone. If it rang while he was in the bathroom or feeding our dogs and cats, I'd grab it before my mom could.

"Is Ace there?" Denny's familiar low voice. According to Dad, Denny bet because he missed playing ball. And because his job was beneath him and his head coach was a dumbass. Denny had called my dad Ace ever since he heard about Dad's pro career.

"He's out," I said. "Who do you like?"

"Cincinnati, Atlanta. Detroit. A dime apiece," he said. A dime was a hundred dollars, making me the middleman in a bet worth three thousand packs of ten-cent Topps baseball cards.

"Got it," I said.

"Say it back."

"Reds, Braves, Tigers, all for a dime."

"Good boy," he said. "Tell your pop I hope I don't bust him too bad."

WHY WAS DAD BOOKING BETS instead of coaching? As a coach, he had turned the Moral Township basketball program from doormat to mini-dynasty. He had done the same at Franklin Central. But it wasn't enough. There was too much downtime. The off-season was too long. There were too many games on TV and radio that meant nothing if he didn't have a bet down. The same bug bit my hustling hero Rose, the Tigers' former 30-game-winner Denny McLain, Colts quarterback Art Schlichter, and others who tried to recapture the rush of their playing days by betting on ballgames. Like them, Dad got ahead of the game from time to time, only to bet more and more until he went bust. People who don't gamble wonder how such a thing can happen. Why not play it safe? Put your profit in a coffee can and play with the rest? Competitors from dice-roller Julius Caesar to Bat Masterson to Titanic Thompson to Michael Jordan could tell you why: for a bet to mean anything, it has to hurt if you lose and change your day if you win. A shiny dime with FDR's head on it can be a wager of consequence to a schoolboy. Jordan might have to risk $50,000 to make the moment matter as much to him. Every other bettor finds a place in between, a number at the crossing of risk and reward. When Dad won a bet on a ninth-inning rally, we slapped hands and danced around his smoky den. When he lost a tough one, he said, "That stings."

His bets varied from fifty to a couple thousand dollars on a given night. When he went bust, he tapped his friends, but they were guys like him, hiding their betting sheets from their wives, hanging up on bill collectors. So he switched jobs. Three times in ten years, he switched school systems, cashed in his pension, and started over. These were teaching posts, not coaching positions, but each move added up to a new bankroll. He was thinking like a ballplayer: a win or two and I'm back in the groove, good as ever. He figured he could always get another coaching job. Meanwhile, he was looking for the cure. That's what he called the one big win he always needed. "I've got the cure for sure," he'd say, marking up his *Gold Sheet*.

Once, flush, he bought a rundown apartment building. Here was long-term security in the form of tenants' rent checks. I helped him paint windowsills, cut the grass, and burn bagworms out of trees at the Troy Plaza Apartments. A year later, he sold the property at a loss. He didn't have the heart to evict elderly residents who couldn't pay their rent. The man who bought the Troy Plaza Apartments from Dad had lost a couple baseball bets and wound up throwing in a pony on top of the purchase price—a fat, sway-backed, foul-tempered creature. Sugar. Dad pictured summer afternoons in the backyard, all the neighborhood kids enjoying pony rides in deep left field. Instead, Sugar bucked. She bit Cathy Lenahan, waited for Cathy to dry her tears and saddle up again, then galloped full speed toward our backyard swing set. It's a good thing Cathy jumped off, or she might have been decapitated.

Dad's soft spot for animals dated back to his father's farm. He liked the barnyard, not the slaughter. At various times, we shared our home with dogs, cats, rabbits, and a pair of pet lizards as well as the pony. Dad didn't cotton to Sugar—nobody did—but he couldn't bring himself to leave her outside in the record-setting cold of 1971, when temperatures sank to eight below. We had no stable, just a yard. "We can't let her freeze," he said. So he led Sugar into the house. The 700-pound harridan stayed in the family room until the freeze broke, eating from a bucket of hay, dropping road apples on the newspapers we spread on the carpet. One evening, we were sitting around the dinner table as my mother said grace. "Bless us, O Lord, and these thy gifts . . ." when the pony began whinnying, kicking the family room door. This wasn't my mother's idea of suburban life. ". . . through Christ our Lord, amen," she said. "The pony has to go."

• • •

DAD SPENT MOST OF MY TEEN YEARS on a losing streak. He said his buddies were beating him "like a drum." He bet with his old bookie, lost more, and then doubled down trying to get even. Sometimes it worked. When it did, he'd limit his betting for a week or so, only to relapse. He found that he could live without new clothes, new shoes, vacations, and premium cigars, but not without action, so he hustled for dimes. At Emmerich Manual High School, on the city's decaying south side, he made a little extra by teaching driver's ed, helping out with the baseball team, and running the library during night school. He'd come home for dinner, then drive back to Manual to tend the library from 6 o'clock to 9:30. I liked to go with him. I took a transistor radio so we could listen to Reds games, WLW's fifty-thousand-watt signal carrying Al Michaels's crisp play-by-play and Joe Nuxhall's homespun stories of his long career with the team.

A quarter century before, Nuxhall had set one of those baseball records that will never be broken. In 1944, the Reds, running short of able-bodied players at the height of World War II, brought the gangly high school freshman to the majors. He was fifteen years and 316 days old, younger than any major-league pitcher before or since. "I'd been pitching against eighth- and ninth-graders. All of a sudden, I look up and there's Stan

184

Musial," Nuxhall said later. On June 10, 1944, with the Reds trailing St. Louis 13–0, manager Bill McKechnie waved the boy to the mound. He got a groundout from Cardinals shortstop George Fallon. Two hits, a wild pitch, and five walks later, McKechnie sent Nuxhall to the leaky showers at Crosley Field. "The Reds sent him down to Birmingham," Dad told me, "and the Birmingham Barons made room on their roster by releasing another left-handed pitcher. Who was it?"

I knew the answer. "You."

On the way to Manual High School, he dropped me off at a Steak 'n Shake nearby. A steakburger and a plate of stringy, salt-crusted fries later, I walked six blocks under sleepy oaks and maples, transistor to my ear, to join him in the library. Sometimes I helped the night school students use the card catalog, a woodgrained warren of drawers full of index cards typed or handwritten with a book's title, author, and Dewey Decimal number, each card corresponding to one of the books on the floor-to-ceiling shelves in what I thought of as Dad's library. On warm nights, we used long wooden poles to open the windows, letting cool air spill over the shelves. One night, the breeze brought a bat in with it. The bat flitted to a spot in a corner of the ceiling and clung there, a dark-furred breathing thing. Several night school students hurried out to the hall. Bats are rabid, they said. Others watched Dad nudge the bat with a window pole. Nothing happened until he found a custodian to help him roll an extra-long ladder into the library. Dad climbed the ladder with a paper bag and bagged the bat. He held the bag out the window, shook it, and the bat flew away.

"Were you scared?" I asked him later.

"You bet. I thought I was going to fall off the ladder."

"What about the bat? Bats are rabid."

"No, he's just a scared little thing that wanted to go home."

Driving back from the library, we heard the end of the Reds game. Announcer Nuxhall had returned to Cincinnati in 1952, the year Dad hurt his arm, and gone on to pitch sixteen seasons in the big leagues. Different careers, but Nuxhall's postgame sign-off suited them both. Dad said it along with the radio: "Here's the old lefthander, rounding third and heading for home."

One afternoon, he was between English classes at Manual. The halls were jammed with students when a fight broke out. Drawn by shouts of "Fight, fight," he saw a boy named Jeff Watts tumble through a glass door. As he hurried to help, kids started screaming. A glass shard protruded from the boy's wrist. The wound was spurting blood. Students and other teachers backed off, but Dad plunged in. Pointing at a boy in the crowd, he said, "Give me your shirt!" Dad used a sleeve to make a tourniquet.

A week later, there was a story in a neighborhood newspaper: "Many may have read of Jeff's accident at Manual High School, when he broke the glass on a swinging door and cut his wrist severely. The family wants to express their deep gratitude to Mr. Cook for saving their boy's life. Had it not been for the competent first aid given by Mr. Arthur B. Cook of the English Department, this could have been a fatal accident."

We never talked much about his heroics that day. My mother's PhD dissertation and my report card were bigger news around the dinner table. I found out years later that the school held a ceremony honoring Dad for saving Jeff Watts's life. It amazes me in retrospect that we didn't make more of it at the time. How many people save a life? Only one that I knew.

HE SHOPPED FOR CLOTHES at the Goodwill Store—ill-fitting slacks, polyester shirts, and a jaunty fedora to cover his bald spot. He used disposable razors until they got so dull and rusted he was practically sawing off his salt-and-pepper whiskers.

I still liked watching ballgames with him, but that didn't keep me from lecturing him about betting. While Dad was nobody's patsy, he was impulsive. He began playing teasers. A teaser is a multipart wager in which you have to win each part to win the bet. In a three-piece parlay, for example, the bettor gets tempting odds or an adjusted line on each of three pieces, but the math is punitive. Teasers are the sort of bet a mobster once defined as "a tax on people who don't under-stand mathematics." Dad, for instance, was sure that he could pick three locks —Tom Seaver, Steve Carlton, and Catfish Hunter, all at home against lousy teams. I explained the ninth-grade math: even if Seaver, Carlton, and Catfish were 80 percent locks, the odds that their teams would win was 0.8 cubed, or 51.2 percent, not enough to cover the vig.

"O ye of no faith," he said. "There's more to it than math. There's heart. There's hunches." He scored on enough hunches to convince himself that he was *this close* to the cure, and the more teasers he played, the more he lost. I began to see him differently. His betting didn't seem so fun when we drove to a blood bank to sell his blood for fifty dollars a pint. Even his blood type, O-negative, was special. It made him a universal donor. His blood cured others and kept him in the game for another night.

There was a night when he didn't come home. My mother wouldn't say why. It turned out that Dad had been arrested as part of a "gambling ring"—him and his friends. He wouldn't name the others, so he spent a night in jail. The next morning, he paid a fine with what was left of his bankroll. Then he sucked up his pride and asked my mother for a loan. She gave him a couple thousand in exchange for control over their bank accounts. From then on, he had to ask for money.

He asked me. I was on my way to college with a student loan in the works. He was at the bottom of his luck. "I could use a little help," he said. Not an easy thing to tell me.

We drove to the bank, where we split my student loan. "I'll pay you back," he said.

"Forget it. You don't have to."

"I'll pay you back."

189

8

★ *Daddy's Girl* ★

JULIA RUTH STEVENS

"They were cheering for Daddy again."

September 9, 2008, was a bright Sunday in the Bronx. The temperature was 75, a whisper of wind blowing out over Monument Park. The Yankees were hosting the Orioles in the 6,581st and final regular-season game at Yankee Stadium.

When the ballpark opened in 1923, John Philip Sousa led his marching band in the national anthem. Babe Ruth christened Yankee Stadium with a game-winning three-run homer. Eighty-five years and twenty-seven World Series championships later, the Yanks were headed for a new home across 161st Street, a sparkling replica of the House That Ruth Built. But the wrecking ball would wait for nine more innings.

Before the game, Whitey Ford and Don Larsen rubbed up a couple of balls with dirt from the pitcher's mound. Yogi Berra, Reggie Jackson, Goose Gossage, Willie Randolph, Paul O'Neill, and Bernie Williams trotted out to their old positions behind Ford and Larsen. Finally, a slim, white-haired woman, a little unsteady on her feet, leaned on her son's arm as he led her onto the field. As she waved to the crowd, announcer Michael Kay introduced her:

"On Opening Day in 1923, Babe Ruth hit the very first home run in the history of this grand stadium. As the stadium's history began with a Ruth, it's only fitting that we close Yankee Stadium with a Ruth. Please welcome the Babe's daughter, Julia Ruth!"

With the image of her father looming on the Jumbotron, ninety-two-year-old Julia stood between the mound and the plate. Rearing back several inches, she lobbed a one-hopper to catcher Jorge Posada.

Fifty thousand fans cheered. A moment later, as starting pitcher Andy Pettitte started for the mound, the ceremonial pitcher followed a superstition older than she was: she took care to step over the first-base line.

Following the game, a 7–3 Pettitte victory over Baltimore, Derek Jeter stood on the mound with a microphone in his hand. "It's a huge honor to put this uniform on," Jeter told the Stadium crowd. "Every member of this organization has been calling this place home for eighty-five years, so there's a lot of tradition here, a lot of history, a lot of memories. The great thing about memories is, you pass them along from generation to generation."

• • •

I DROVE TO LAS VEGAS to meet the Babe's adopted daughter in April 2014. Speeding through the Hualipai and Aquarius mountains, past Joshua trees and tumbleweed, and then down from the mountains toward the shrinking blue of thirsty Lake Mead, I listened to sports-talk radio reports on the Diamondbacks' dismal pitching and the Yankees' $209 million payroll. The Yanks had made an off-season splash by signing Japanese starter Masahiro Tanaka for $22 million a year, plus a $20 million fee to his team in Japan. But their offense was sluggish. A radio host said they needed "a basher. And I'm not talking A-Rod. I'm talking the Yankees of old. I'm talking Reggie," said the radio voice. "Mantle and Maris. Joe D and Lou Gehrig, all the way back to the greatest of them all. You know who I mean. The Bambino. What was it they called him? The king of . . . the somethin' of swat."

Henderson, Nevada, on the southeast outskirts of Vegas, is a warren of chain restaurants, third-rate casinos, and gas stations. Boys on bikes and skateboards ride the sidewalks past two-story, two-garage stucco homes like the one where I found the Sultan of Swat's daughter.

Julia Ruth Stevens, now ninety-seven, offered a hand as light as a bird's wing. Legally blind, she turned her head to get a glimpse of me. "There you are," she said. "I've still got some peripheral vision, you know." She was dressed for our talk in tan slacks and a floral blouse. A large brass cross dangled from her neck. She had put on a dab of lipstick and a touch of rouge on her cheeks. Her only extravagance was the ring on her left hand, a horseshoe of diamonds. When I said I was glad to meet her, she said she was glad to meet anyone. "Every day I wake up is a pleasant surprise."

Macular degeneration in both eyes forces her to squint to see outlines of the photos and posters of Ruth on the walls: Babe swinging for the fences, chatting with Ted Williams, waving to a grandstand full of fans. Her vision is sharpest, she said, when she shuts her eyes. That's when she's a girl again, sitting in a box seat at the old stadium.

Most of us see Babe Ruth in the grainy grays of old photos and newsreels. Not Julia. When she shuts her eyes, she sees a high blue sky over the Bronx in the 1930s, the sun so bright it whitens the tips of the shiny green grass as her father steps to the plate, tipping his cap to his little girl. Those memories impelled her to take up a new hobby in 2004, the year she turned eighty-eight. Throwing out the first pitch at a ballgame is her way of keeping her family in the game. At a time when many young fans, players, and sports talkers have only a hazy idea of who Babe Ruth was, she wants to remind them that, in his time, he *was* baseball. "I'm certainly not trying to impress anyone with my throwing, even if I could," she says. "It's about keeping Daddy's memory alive."

THE MOST CELEBRATED AMERICAN OF HIS TIME, George Herman Ruth turned the old slap-and-dash pastime of Honus Wagner and Ty Cobb into a spectacle that transfixed the nation in the years between world wars.

The Babe's father, a Baltimore saloonkeeper known as Big George, once tried a more respectable trade, selling lightning rods. He waited for thunderstorms that never came. Nobody who knew Big George was surprised: he was no businessman. Money slipped through his hands like beer from a spigot. His wife died young and their son spent more time in his father's tavern, euphemistically called Ruth's Café, than he ever spent in school. He drank. He stole. At the age of ten, the "incorrigible" child was sent to St. Mary's Industrial School for Boys, a reform school where he grew tall and strong, with a round face, a wide nose, and a full mouth that led his reform school inmates to call him "Nigger Lips." Still, he was popular among the boys and the Xaverian brothers who ran St. Mary's, for a simple reason: he was the best teen pitcher Baltimore had ever seen. The best hitter, too. The kid could hit the ball out of sight. At the time, however, hitting home runs was no more than a sideshow in a sport that emphasized speed, bunts, and hit-and-run plays.

In 1914, the nineteen-year-old Ruth joined the minor-league Baltimore Orioles, who soon sold him to the big-league Boston Red Sox.

Two years later, at age twenty-one, left-handed hurler Ruth won 23 games and lost 12 for the Red Sox, with a league-leading 1.75 earned run average. In 1918, he had an ERA of 2.22 while batting .300 and tying for the major-league home-run crown with 11. In three years on the mound, he won 65 games with a 2.02 ERA, and he was even better in the postseason: three wins, no losses, and a historic stretch of 29⅔ scoreless World Series innings, a record that stood until Whitey Ford broke it more than forty years later.

"Daddy was always quite proud of his pitching," Julia recalls. "He liked to remind the writers, 'I was a pretty fair pitcher for six years.' "

But Ruth was a genius with a bat in his hands. In 1909, Ty Cobb led the major leagues with nine home runs. Five years later, the Philadelphia Athletics' Frank "Home Run" Baker paced the still-young American League with nine of his own. Five years after that, in 1919, the Red Sox' pie-faced left fielder, George "Babe" Ruth, became an everyday player for the first time. He batted .322 and led the American League with a record 29 home runs. The rest of Boston's roster combined for four, bringing the team total to 33 homers. A year later, Ruth became the first to hit 30 home runs in a season. He was the first to hit

40 homers, the first to hit 50, the first to hit 60, all in the span of nine magical seasons with the Yankees, who bought his contract from Boston after his breakthrough season in 1919. In those nine years, he remade baseball in his own image. Even today, almost seventy years after his death, Babe Ruth is the biggest name in baseball history.

In 1921, Ruth batted .378 with 59 homers and 168 RBIs. He scored 177 runs, stole 17 bases, and reached base well over half the time he came to the plate. He had ten other years that were almost as good. Was it a more primitive era, a game played by fewer outstanding athletes? Yes and no. The best players of his day were probably no worse than today's stars. Two experiments clocked Walter Johnson's fastball at an average of 99.7 miles per hour. There's little reason to think Ty Cobb couldn't hit .300 today, or that a modern Ruth wouldn't hit 40 to 50 home runs.

Almost as famed for his appetites as for his hitting, Ruth could gobble four hot dogs in eight bites. He enjoyed illegal Prohibition liquor in more gulps than that, downing half a dozen beers and a bottle of Scotch during a night on the town, then going three-for-four the next after-noon. One writer recorded a Ruthian breakfast: an eighteen-egg omelet, three servings of ham, half a loaf of buttered toast, and a pot of coffee. His nighttime exploits were legendary, too. Ping Bodie, one of his Yankees roommates, said, "I

don't room with him, I room with his suitcase."
According to Ruth biographer Robert Creamer,
"He was very noisy in bed, visceral grunts and
gasps and whoops accompanying his erotic
exertions." Creamer quotes a friend who called the
Bambino "the noisiest fucker in North America."
This was no way to impress the men who ran
baseball. Yankees owner Jacob Ruppert never
forgot the morning—or was it early afternoon?—
when he woke New York's hero by yanking the
covers off Ruth and a paid companion.

In the media world of the 1920s, a Catholic like
Babe Ruth couldn't afford to project the image
of a skirt-chasing tomcat. To keep up appearances,
he needed a wife.

As a Red Sox rookie, he'd met a shy, pretty
waitress in a Boston coffee shop. Helen Woodward
was nineteen when they married in the fall of
1914. So was her bridegroom, but he never made
much of a husband. As his career took off, the
Babe blazed a trail through the beds of willing
women in American League cities. When he got
one of his mistresses pregnant, she gave birth to
a daughter they named Dorothy. Married seven
years and still childless, Helen adopted Dorothy.
Within a year, however, finally tired of her
husband's infidelities, she moved out and took
the child with her.

Soon, Ruth crossed paths with a young widow
from Athens, Georgia. Claire Hodgson had once

had a flirtation with Ty Cobb before marrying and giving birth to a daughter, Julia. After her hard-drinking husband died, Claire borrowed a hundred dollars from an uncle, packed up, and took a train to New York, where she went in search of work with her toddler at her side. One day, she rapped on Howard Chandler Christy's door. Christy was the Alberto Vargas of his day, an illustrator who sold racy paintings to glossy magazines. He took one look at little Julia and said, "Good God, don't tell me it's one of mine."

Claire assured Christy that she was only looking for a job. He told her about a casting call, which led to work on a Broadway chorus line. She caught Ruth's eye, and they began dining together, but apparently not sleeping together. Biographer Creamer describes Claire's "beautiful dark hair, snapping dark eyes, pert face, red lips, and superb figure," calling her "the epitome of early twentieth-century glamour: a beautiful young widow." But there was no talk of marriage; Ruth's religion wouldn't allow him to divorce Helen.

Babe had lost touch with his estranged wife. In 1929, he learned that she had been living with a dentist in Watertown, Massachusetts, calling the man her husband. The dentist had wired their home with faulty fuses, and that winter the fuses caused a fire. He was out that night. Daughter Dorothy was staying with friends. Helen died in a blaze so destructive that her body was found near a second-story radiator that had fallen through the floor.

After the fire, widower Ruth was free to wed again. After three months of public mourning, the thirty-four-year-old Bambino married twenty-eight-year-old Claire Hodgson at the Church of St. Gregory the Great on West 90th Street in New York. It was April 17, Opening Day of the 1929 season, with the Yanks scheduled to host the Red Sox that afternoon. Babe, hoping to duck reporters and fans, paid the parish priest to perform the ceremony at 5:45 in the morning, but word got out. By the time he and Claire drove up in his half-ton Packard a little before sunrise, hundreds of fans, reporters, and neighborhood boys stood on the church steps, waiting in the rain. "Hello, boys," said Ruth, leading Claire up the steps.

After the service, the newlyweds returned to his twelve-room apartment on Riverside Drive. The rain kept falling as goodwill and bootleg liquor flowed, and soon the Babe took a happy phone call. "Ho ho, we're rained out!" he announced to dozens of friends and well-wishers.

The party lasted all night. A day later, for the first time, Claire entered Yankee Stadium as Mrs. Babe Ruth. She sat in a field-level box near the home dugout, cheering her new husband as he clouted a homer in a Yanks victory. Rounding third, he tipped his cap to Claire and blew her a kiss. His teammates razzed him about that. From then on, whenever they saw Claire in the box seats, they blew him kisses. He laughed and blew kisses right back.

Julia was twelve when her mother married the most famous man in America. "My, how things changed," she told me eighty-five years later.

Babe and Claire combined families in the Upper West Side apartment. He adopted Julia. Claire adopted seven-year-old Dorothy, who returned to her father's household. Dorothy and Julia lived as sisters, with Julia attending the elite Rayson School for Girls and then the Tisné Institute, a finishing school where she wore silk suits and satin blouses while perfecting her posture and studying French. Claire ran the house, reining in her husband's spending. "He was generous to a fault," Julia says. "If some old ballplayer asked for a hundred-dollar loan, he'd say, 'Sure, here's two hundred!' Mother put a stop to that." Claire capped her husband's expenses by writing him fifty-dollar checks, and when the cancelled checks came back from the bank with his signature on them, she sold them to autograph collectors for a dollar or two.

"She's a smart one," Ruth said of Claire. He didn't mind the discipline she imposed. He still enjoyed a drink or three, but with a wife and two girls to look after, he drank less. He smoked cigars and dipped chaw, but not as much as before. With Claire looking over his shoulder, he could forget about money and focus on hitting. In 1930, the thirty-five-year-old Bambino batted .359 with 49 homers and 153 RBIs. In the top-this phrases of the day, the Sultan of Swat was now also the Bazoo of Bang, the Maharajah of Mash, the Wizard of Whack. "Wherever we went, the crowd worshipped him because he was Babe Ruth," Julia says. "I worshipped him, too, because he was my daddy."

It was a fifteen-minute drive from the Ruths' apartment to Yankee Stadium. "He'd drive us to the game in his sixteen-cylinder Cadillac coupe, Mother and Daddy in the front seat, me in the back," Julia remembers. Ruth drove fast, and if traffic got heavy, he sometimes detoured onto sidewalks. "Motorcycle cops would pull him over, looking very stern, but when they saw who it was, they'd say, 'Where you going, Babe? Follow me!' And we got a police escort to the game."

Unlike other kids, she never asked Ruth to hit a home run for her, but each time he came to bat, she would shut her eyes and hope for one, whispering, "Hit that apple in the eye, and then you'll see how far it'll fly!" But Julia's ballpark memories are outnumbered by homier ones. "When I remember him, he's not in his uniform. He's in a sport shirt, coming through the door front door, looking for a hug."

Teammates often joined him for postgame

drinks and dinner. Julia remembers Lefty Gomez, who kicked like a Rockette to start his windup on the mound. Gomez had a big, long nose and a quick grin. Skinny second baseman Tony Lazzeri had bags under his eyes that made him look like he never slept. Sometimes Hoagy Carmichael and Jack Dempsey dropped by. Both of them played the piano, Dempsey croaking along as he thumped the keys. And then there was gentle Lou Gehrig, the college man from Columbia who called Ruth his hero. In the off-season, Ruth and Gehrig hunted and fished together. Still, Lou seldom stayed for dinner at the Ruths' apartment. While the other men scarfed down Claire's ham and cabbage, the Iron Horse went home for dinner to New Rochelle, where he lived with his parents. "Lou was a bit of a stick in the mud," says Julia.

Even after curbing her husband's spending, Claire Ruth frowned on Gehrig's penny-pinching. "Babe could be ridiculous, leaving a ten-dollar tip where fifty cents would have been generous, but Lou's dimes were just as silly," she said.

In 1931, a spat between the Ruth and Gehrig women spilled into the Yanks' dugout. One day that summer, Dorothy, who was something of a tomboy, spent the morning playing at the Gehrigs' house. Dorothy was always climbing fences and trees, skinning her knees, scuffing and tearing her dresses. Julia, five years older, wore more sophisticated clothes and had outgrown playtime. Lou's mother, known to all as Mom Gehrig, shook her head at Dorothy's clothing. "A shame how that woman dresses those girls," she said of Claire. "There's poor Dorothy in tatters, but her own daughter's in satin and silk."

Her comment made its way back to Riverside Drive. According to Julia, "Mother had steam coming out of her ears. She told Daddy, 'You tell Lou his mother had better keep her nose out of my cotton-picking business!'"

Before the next day's game, Ruth did just that. And for once, Gehrig got angry. The Iron Horse, ordinarily the mildest of men, would not hear a cross word about his mother. Never the type to raise his voice, he leaned toward Ruth and said, "Don't ever speak to me again, except on the ball field." From that day until Ruth's retirement in 1935, Gehrig froze him out. After a Ruthian homer, he would ignore Babe as he rounded the bases and touched the plate, leaving the number-five hitter—Lazzeri or outfielder Ben Chapman—to shake Ruth's hand.

Not even feuding with Gehrig dampened Ruth's spirits. Restless on a rainy afternoon, he'd take Julia's hand. "Let's go bowling!" Hurling left-handed fastballs that sent pins flying—and sent boy pinsetters ducking for cover—he often scored 200 or better while finishing-school student Julia, proper as ever, rolling the ball with ladylike posture as if she were balancing a book on her head, plinked enough pins to made Daddy proud. "You're pretty darned good!" he'd say in his booming baritone. When she came down with a nasty strep throat and needed a transfusion, he was her blood donor. "After that, I didn't feel adopted anymore," she says. "I felt we were blood relatives, because I had his blood in my veins."

At home, they made one-eyed eggs: he'd brown a slice of toast in a frying pan, cut a hole in the middle, and drop an egg into it, then add a slice of fried bologna. They listened to his favorite radio thrillers, *The Lone Ranger*, *The Green Hornet*, and *Gangbusters*. She would curl up at his feet as Ruth sat in his favorite chair, facing a double window that looked out over the Hudson. "At Christmas, we'd go up Broadway to the stores that sold Christmas trees. He'd pick one out and set it up in the living room. He'd put all the ornaments on it, all the little electric lights. He walked around the tree, placing tin-foil icicles on the branches, one strand at a time. Then he'd turn on the Christmas-tree lights, and we'd sit in the darkened room, looking at the tree. Oh, how beautiful!"

Julia puts her hands to her face as if to hold in the memory. Her ring catches the light. The ring was once a diamond stickpin Ruth wore. Claire thought it was gaudy. The stickpin appears in vintage photos and in Creamer's biography: "Before he met Claire he had worn extravagantly expensive clothes, loud garish things including a diamond horseshoe tie pin."

On Julia's eighteenth birthday, in 1934, her parents gave her a diamond horseshoe ring made from the tie pin. The ring has been on her hand ever since.

In those days, young men would summon up the courage to ring the doorbell and introduce themselves to Mr. Ruth. He shook their quivering hands and said, "Hiya, kid. Get my girl back home by ten, you hear?" The boys took Julia out for sodas or milkshakes, or to Palisades Amusement Park across the river, with its roller coaster and saltwater swimming pool, and never failed to get her home by ten.

One boy was special. "He asked me to marry him, and I said yes." But her parents said no. "They said I was crazy, too young to get married." Julia broke off the engagement and joined her parents on a cruise that played a role in her daddy's future heartbreak. The cruise took the Ruths to Hawaii, where Babe schmoozed with actor Spencer Tracy and Duke Kahanamoku, founding father of surfing, on Waikiki Beach. The Babe was no Sultan of Surf: he kept slipping off his board, but Julia made it to her feet for a golden moment on one of the Duke's longboards, her daddy applauding as if she'd hit a home run.

In the end, that trip meant more than any of them realized.

As Ruth's historic career wound down, he announced that he wanted to manage the Yankees. The idea struck many as laughable. Jacob Ruppert, the wealthy brewer who owned the Yankees, chided the skirt-chasing boozehound he called Root. "How could you manage others, Root, when you can't manage yourself?" In time, though, Ruppert seemed to reconsider. Twice he let Ruth believe he was about to become player-manager, only to hire someone else.

"Who else knows more about the game than me?" the Babe fumed to reporters. "I don't think Mr. Ruppert realizes I have matured. I'm a grown man with a family, not the playboy I was in 1919." Who else had been a star pitcher *and* hitter in the majors? Not Cobb, Hornsby, or any of the other immortals. And who knew more about the temptations ballplayers face? Still, he was passed over again and again. The Red Sox, White Sox, and Tigers considered making Ruth a player-manager, only to hire men he saw as lesser fellows. In 1935, after several discussions with Ruth, the Red Sox purchased All-Star shortstop Joe Cronin from the Senators and made him player-manager. Cronin was only twenty-eight.

Reporters said someone upstairs disliked Babe Ruth. That someone was Judge Kenesaw Mountain Landis, the commissioner who had assumed dictatorial powers in the wake of the 1919 Black Sox Scandal. The flinty Landis saw the great Bambino as a throwback to more freewheeling times. During one dispute over a barnstorming tour, he fined and suspended Ruth, saying, "I'll show that big baboon who's running this game."

Ruth laughed it off. "Aw, tell the old guy to jump in a lake."

Just before the Ruths' cruise to Hawaii, Detroit owner Frank Navin decided to make Babe Ruth player-manager of the Tigers. All the new manager had to do was take an overnight train to Detroit to sign his contract. Yet Ruth put him off. "I'm taking my girls on a cruise. I'll call Navin when I get back," he told Yankees general manager Ed Barrow.

Barrow said, "You're making a mistake."

"C'mon. The season doesn't begin for six months," Ruth said.

Navin wouldn't wait. While the Babe fell off surfboards at Waikiki Beach, the Tigers' owner bought catcher Mickey Cochrane from Connie Mack's Athletics and made Cochrane the Tigers' player-manager.

Meanwhile, Mack was thinking about stepping down as manager of the Athletics. A year after selling Cochrane, he named Ruth player-manager of a barnstorming club that toured Japan, an all-star squad featuring Gehrig, Gomez, and Jimmie Foxx. The Babe's knowledge of the game impressed the old man, but Mack didn't like the bad blood between Gehrig and Ruth. Mack also worried about Ruth's troubles with Commissioner Landis, and he thought Ruth seemed a little hen-pecked. "I couldn't make Babe manager," he said. "His wife would have been running the club in a month." Mack, who was seventy-one, returned as the Athletics' manager in 1935 and kept the job for fifteen more years.

"IT'S HELL TO GET OLDER," Ruth said. At the age of forty, he returned to Boston, signing with the lowly Boston Braves after owner Emil Fuchs promised to make him the manager in a season or two. But when Ruth didn't hit, Fuchs forgot his promise. In 28 games with the Braves, Ruth batted .181 with six home runs, lifting his career total to 714. He retired in 1935.

"For years after that, he would come through the door with a question," Julia says. "'Did the phone ring?'" They all knew what that meant. Claire was the one who had to tell him no.

Ruth and Gehrig finally made up on the Fourth of July, 1939. That was the day Gehrig, aged thirty-six and dying of ALS, said goodbye at Yankee Stadium. "Today, I consider myself the luckiest man on the face of the earth," he told the teary crowd. "I might have been given a bad break, but I've got an awful lot to live for." In one account, fifty thousand fans cheered for two minutes as "Gehrig turned to look, almost as if for approval, to his estranged former teammate. The Babe responded by giving Lou a giant hug."

Gehrig died in 1941. Ruth lived another seven years—mostly happy years, his daughter says, "except for that one thing." The best player of his time, maybe the best of any time, never managed an inning of major-league ball. When the Yankees ignored him again in 1946, choosing Bucky Harris instead, "Daddy sat down and cried." Julia believes that being snubbed "broke his heart." She also believes she knows an underlying reason for his heartbreak.

"He said it was a shame that Negroes weren't allowed to play." Ruth had barnstormed with Negro League stars like Satchel Paige, Josh Gibson, Oscar Charleston, and Cool Papa Bell on tours that were boycotted by white reporters and many white ballplayers. According to Bill Jenkinson, one of his biographers, Ruth wanted to help black players "knock down the color barrier" as early as 1920. "And he was always talking about Satchel Paige," Julia says. "Oh, he thought Paige was just great." The Babe's black friends included dancer Bill "Bojangles" Robinson, who would serve as a pallbearer at his funeral. "Judge Landis, unfortunately, was a bigot, and he knew that if Daddy got to manage, he'd want to bring in Negro players." There was no rule barring black players, only a gentleman's agreement among the game's executives. It wasn't until three years after Landis died that his successor, A. B. "Happy" Chandler, approved Jackie Robinson's contract with the Brooklyn Dodgers.

Folding her hands in her lap, Julia says, "Daddy might have done it years earlier. I believe he would have tried." If she's right, Babe Ruth might have helped a black player break baseball's color line a decade or more before Robinson did it in 1947.

TWICE WIDOWED, Julia Ruth Stevens has outlived "just about everybody." Her mother died in 1976, sister Dorothy in 1989. She lives in Nevada with her son, Tom, and his wife, Anita. They hope to move to Hawaii, but it's expensive to live there. "I'm anything but rich," Julia says. Aside from the horseshoe diamond ring, she has hardly any Babe Ruth memorabilia. The Yankees jersey on the living-room wall is a replica. So is a beer poster that shows Ruth swatting a homer. "After Daddy died, men from the Hall of Fame came around, asking for bats and balls and uniforms. Mother told them to take what they wanted. She didn't know they'd take almost everything."

Other Ruth relics found their way into private hands. In 1997, Yankees pitcher David Wells paid $35,000 for a Yanks hat signed by the Babe, the most ever paid for a baseball cap. Wells, sporting a Ruth tattoo on his pitching arm, wore the cap for an inning that season, held on to it for fifteen years, and sold it in 2012 for $537,278. Also in 2012, a jersey Ruth wore during his first Yankees season sold for $4.4 million. That was $1.6 million more than the 1909 Honus Wagner baseball card that was once the holy grail of memorabilia. It was $100,000 more than a collector recently paid for the original thirteen rules of basketball typewritten by James Naismith, making Ruth's jersey the most expensive sports souvenir ever. Ruthabilia is the most valuable kind of sports memorabilia, worth hundreds of millions of dollars all told, and his heirs have hardly any of it.

When Claire Ruth died in 1976, she left behind a cedar chest that held a couple of her husband's home and road uniforms. Julia gave the cedar chest away. Today, its contents could be worth $10 million. Julia's son, Tom, gave other mementos to charities and family friends. "We had no idea how much those old things might be worth," he says. They saw them the way Ruth and his widow did, as a bunch of grimy old bats and balls and shirts, stuff nobody would want. The Babe's family shared that view with many others of their time. Famous players' autographs always had value, but who imagined that dirty old equipment, rebranded as memorabilia, would someday be auctioned off for millions of dollars?

Who knew that collectors would pay for the very dirt ballplayers walked on?

Some families were more sentimental. They hung on to Dad's old gloves, scrapbooks, and other souvenirs. Whether they stowed them in the garage or displayed them in a trophy room, the idea was to celebrate his playing days. (One player, showing me through his den, with its framed jerseys, trophies, and magazine covers under track lights, called it "the typical tacky trophy room.") And when he died, they had those keepsakes to remember him by.

As years passed and the memorabilia market grew, a fortunate few faced a dilemma. If Dad or Granddad was a Hall of Famer, his bat or his cap might be worth thousands of dollars. When, if ever, should they sell?

Julia was both lucky and unlucky in that department. Almost anything belonging to Ruth gained value over the years, but due to her mother's generosity to the Hall of Fame and others who came asking after the Babe died, she got next to none of it. Other than the diamond on her finger, there was a watch the Yankees gave Ruth when he retired and a handful of trinkets nobody would bid on. The fact that she had so little of her father's stuff made her treasure what she had even more. Julia swore she wouldn't sell her diamond ring at any price because it served a purpose beyond price. Like many heirlooms, almost like a religious relic, it helped keep her daddy alive—not, in this case, to the fans, but to her.

Today, the Hall of Fame has far more Ruth mementos than it can display. The Bambino looms over the Hall like no other player: a huge photo overlooking the membership desk; a giant photorealistic portrait at the entrance to the Art Gallery; a life-sized statue near his plaque in the rotunda. The second-floor Ruth Room, the only room devoted to a single player, is one of the Hall's most popular exhibits. I told curator Tom Shieber and Hall of Fame spokesman Craig Muder about Julia's plight. "She's got hardly anything of his. Her mother gave it away, much of it to the Hall. What if you gave one of her dad's old bats back to Julia?"

They looked at me as if I'd suggested a yard sale. "Not possible," they explained. The Hall of Fame is a nonprofit institution that gets no share of Major League Baseball's billions. The Hall has money problems of its own. And suppose they gave Julia a bat she could sell for a million dollars—how long before every relative of every Hall of Famer came asking for a bat or some other priceless artifact. "Imagine the snowball effect!" Muder said. I'd pictured a quieter transfer—an assistant curator slipping a bat or a hat out of one of the Hall of Fame's three climate-controlled warehouses and giving it to Julia, who could say,

"I found this in the basement!" But the Hall of Fame isn't in the regifting business. It holds legal title to its artifacts. It preserves them on behalf of the game and its fans and reserves the right to display them, even those that are currently in storage. Muder mentioned another hitch: any items that went from Cooperstown to the memorabilia market might sell for more due to their Hall of Fame provenance, turning the Hall into a feeder system for Steiner Sports and eBay. "Is that what we want to do with the game's history?" Despite what the Babe might have wanted, his bats, gloves, caps, jerseys, shoes, trophies, contracts, golf clubs, Yankee Stadium locker, and other possessions were staying in Cooperstown. At least Julia still had the ring he and Claire gave her on her eighteenth birthday.

Julia never played baseball or softball. She considered herself a bit of a klutz. It was only later in life that the game exerted a familiar pull on her. Passing a Little League game, she would turn to see better with her peripheral vision. Not for the hits and errors but for the way the players moved and the sounds they made. The umpire's strike call, the crack of the bat, and the cheers all reminded her of her daddy. At the same time, she worried that he was fading from the game's collective memory. Roger Maris broke his single-season record of 60 homers in 1961. Hank Aaron broke Ruth's career home-run record in 1974.

Julia thought Aaron seemed a nice enough fellow. So did Barry Bonds, who received baseball's annual Babe Ruth Award for his 73 homers in 2001. Yet she was convinced that her daddy was better than any of them. Given the game's evolution—more teams, more games, closer fences on the road, empty "hitters' backgrounds" in the center-field seats that were crowded with white shirts in Ruth's day, plus a livelier-than-ever ball—"I think that if he played today, he might hit 75 home runs."

To keep his name alive, Julia became a one-pitch pitcher. She had hardly ever thrown a ball, but starting in 2004 she began throwing out ceremonial first pitches at ballgames all over the country. "It was a way of keeping Daddy's name out there. I was terribly nervous the first time," she told me, "but somehow the ball got to the catcher."

Accepting a glass of water from her daughter-in-law, she apologized for sounding tired. And for the mess. The living room was strewn with cardboard boxes. The Stevenses were packing up to go to Hawaii, still hoping they could afford it. Julia's son, Tom, a civil engineer who helped the U.S. military build bridges in Afghanistan's Uruzgan province, had agreed to take a job in Honolulu. Such a move would make it harder for Julia to throw ceremonial pitches on the mainland. "I want to keep doing that as long as I can." Still, she hoped the move would happen. She hadn't been to Hawaii since the family cruise in 1933, but could still see her daddy on the beach at Waikiki, tumbling off his surfboard, applauding when she hung ten for a second.

That wasn't the only applause she remembered. "Do you know what I really liked about throwing out the first pitch in New York? When all the people cheered, it wasn't really for me. I thought they were cheering for Daddy again."

Las Vegas–area real estate prices had plunged after the crash of 2008. Her son was scrambling to sell his house to pay for the move to Hawaii. Finally, a few days after my visit, Tom Stevens decided to auction off the watch the Yankees gave his grandfather when they retired his number, a Longines pocket watch inscribed BABE RUTH—SILVER ANNIVERSARY—YANKEE STADIUM 1923–1948 'THE HOUSE THAT RUTH BUILT.' The firm handling the sale told Tom that the watch should fetch $750,000. For Julia and her family, that would change everything.

9

★ *The Dad Report* ★

ART COOK, LATE INNINGS

In 1975, I went off to college at Butler University, Dad's alma mater. I came home on holidays to find the old backstop leaning sideways like a drunk, a frayed net hanging from the driveway hoop. Dad was a diminished figure by then. He taught driver's ed and ran the night school library at Manual High School, but couldn't land a coaching job. There were too many questions about his abrupt departures from other schools, his beat-up cars, thrift-shop clothing, and general air of decline. Summer nights, he sat in a rusted-out Mercury Cougar in the driveway, smoking a cigarillo, listening to ballgames on the radio.

He looked older than his years, like someone life had bypassed. I figured I had passed him by, too. Then, in 1976, one of his former basketball players became principal at Triton Central High in rural Shelby County. The young man offered Dad the head-coaching job at tiny Triton, half an hour from Indianapolis. And so Art Cook returned to the hothouse gyms of Shelby County, where fans remembered him as the handsome young coach who'd led Moral Township to the best seasons in school history twenty years before. Suddenly, his picture was in newspapers again. The job didn't pay much, but he bought a new pair of glasses to replace the pair he'd held together with a Band-Aid. Re-energized, competitive as ever, he led Triton's Tigers to their first championship in nine years. The *Indianapolis Star* hailed "Cook, a big winner at Franklin Central more than a decade ago, who celebrated his return to coaching at Triton Central by knocking off Morristown for the Shelby County title."

Two years later, the winningest coach in school history left Triton to return to Indianapolis, where the money was better. He took a teaching job at a middle school, where he coached twelve-year-olds in an empty gym.

After college, I was hired as an editor at *Playboy* magazine in Chicago—the world's best job, according to my friends back home. My duties included interviewing Playmates of the Month, sometimes at Hugh Hefner's California mansion. Pamela Anderson told Hef she despised me because my Playmate story made her sound promiscuous, but I kept the job and eventually got to write about sports. Though *Playboy* was known for its foot-ball coverage, it hadn't paid much attention to baseball, and that beat eventually fell to me. For ten years, I wrote the magazine's annual baseball preview, attending the winter meetings and spring training in Florida and Arizona, spending long afternoons at Wrigley Field and other ballparks, talking to players, coaches, managers, scouts, fans, and reporters. The annual preview featured my predictions for World Series champions. A few of those teams finished last, and I may have helped put the Montreal Expos out of business. Right or wrong, I learned something from every baseball man I met, but never connected the dots between Dad's pitching career and my work. I just thought I had a feel for the game.

During my first year at *Playboy*, I fell for a Chicago girl. Pamela Marin, twenty-three years old, dark-haired, sharp-witted, was working her way from the secretarial pool into the talent pool of *Playboy* contributors. Pamela liked Dad, and vice versa. Aside from her looks, he liked her directness. "She says what she thinks."

Pamela wondered how he had gotten sidelined in his own life. "He reminds me of what I like about you," she said.

"That I'm genetically predisposed to have a huge stomach when I'm sixty?"

"Of course that's a major turn-on. But I'm thinking more along the lines of: he's funny. And kind. I'd trust him with my life."

She encouraged me to call him. At first, my

calls were obligatory. "How are you doing? How's the weather? How 'bout the Reds?" But he usually said something that stuck with me.

After I hung up the phone one day, Pamela found me staring out the window. "He thinks teams should double-steal more," I told her. "It's a better bet than a straight steal. Even if they throw one guy out, you always gain a base. Usually, you gain two."

"What do you think?" she asked.

"He's right."

Little by little, we brought him into our lives, helping spur a late-life comeback for Dad. We arranged for him to meet Morganna, the buxom "Kissing Bandit" who ran onto the field to kiss All-Stars, and she planted a smooch on Dad's cheek. We drove from Chicago to Indianapolis, where Pamela nicknamed his belly the Hoosier Dome, and spent an occasional weekend with him and my mother. We shot baskets in the drive-way and watched televised ballgames together. Once, when Dad called a series of pitches in advance—"Fastball on the hands . . . slider low and away . . . fastball up"—Pamela asked if we were watching a rerun of the game. I said, "No, he does that all the time." He wasn't always right, but sometimes he predicted six or seven pitches in a row.

One weekend, Dad brought a dusty trash bag upstairs from the basement. Inside was his scrapbook. Paging through its yellowed, crinkling pages, I found a handsome young Art Cook scattering footnotes to baseball history. He faced Gil Hodges, fanned Eddie Mathews, surrendered that Ted Kluszewski homer that went into orbit, got released by the Birmingham Barons to make roster room for teenager Joe Nuxhall. One page in the scrapbook showed a *Kingston Whig-Standard* story on a Joe DiMaggio grand slam. Beside it was a photo of Dad under the headline ART COOK WINS 21ST GAME—GREAT LEFTHANDER HURLS DOUBLE BILL. According to the story, "Art Cook, greatest lefthander in the Border League, turned in his 21st victory of the season when the Ponies blanked the Ogdensburg Maples . . . Cook's brilliant shutout effort in the opener and the courage he exhibited in the next game were highlights of the show. In winning 21 games he performed a remarkable feat and it was fitting that during the intermission he was given a watch." That doubleheader didn't count as one of his Iron Man stunts because he lost the second game. I never found out what happened to the watch.

Another page held an ad for Art Cook Appreciation Night at Kingston's Megaffin Stadium in 1948, when fans saluted the league's great left-hander. Just as he'd always remembered, he got shelled in the third inning. Then, near the back of the scrapbook, I found this story from an off-season sports page: "Art Cook, one of the most popular players ever to wear the colors of the Kingston Ponies . . . is keenly awaiting the opening of the baseball season and has announced that he will be one of the first to report to the Ponies for spring training. It will be recalled that he arrived in midsummer in 1949 and gave his best in a losing cause despite the fact that his hurling arm had been beset by injuries."

I wrote a column about Dad's scrapbook for *Sports Illustrated*. The piece made him a star to his betting buddies and a hero to my sportswriter friends, who quizzed him about his pro days and his views on everything from beanballs to steroids. Reporters from Kingston and other towns where he'd played called to interview him. I tried getting Dad into the Indiana Baseball Hall of Fame along with Hodges, Three-Finger Brown, and Kenesaw Mountain Landis. The Hall wouldn't admit a career minor leaguer, but it displayed the *SI* column about him.

By then, my magazine friends and I were members of one of the first fantasy baseball leagues. Our league's founder, Rob Fleder, had been a founding father of the original Rotisserie League. When he jumped from *Esquire* to *Playboy* a year later, he brought the idea to Chicago.

Rotisserie League Baseball, granddaddy of all fantasy sports, was born in New York in 1980. The founders were publishing types: editor and author Daniel Okrent, author Harry Stein, editor Peter Gethers, publisher Valerie Salembier, and half a dozen others concocted the idea at a Manhattan bistro, La Rotisserie Française. Two principles were crucial. First, team "owners" used real money to draft major-league players, whose real-life stats determined which Rotisserie owner won the pennant. Second, teams had to have screwy names. Okrent's Fenokees competed with the Stein Brenners, Salembier Flambés, and operatically inclined Fleder Mice. Two years after the original league's big bang, our Great Lakes Bush League became the third in fantasy history. We never dreamed the hobby would boom into a $10 billion business with thirty-four million U.S. players, leaving Rob and the other founders wishing they had found a way to patent the idea. (They did protect the name Rotisserie Baseball, which all those millions of players have had the good sense not to use.) But the hobby helped turn Dad's life around.

After I helped him set up Indiana's first fantasy-sports league, Commissioner Cook held court with his Indy East League cronies at a neighborhood restaurant, the Anchor Inn. I smuggled him tips from big-league locker rooms and his team, the Dads, dominated. He made it up to the losers by sending them free copies of his son's magazine, *Playboy*.

Pamela and I were married by then. When she landed a job as a feature writer for the *Orange County Register*, I followed her to Southern California. Knocking out freelance magazine stories, I checked in with Dad if I was writing about a ballplayer. "Is he a gamer?" he'd ask, and I realized that my heroes were people who never quit and never complained. That's a gamer—someone who gets the job done. Someone who works hard with no fuss, without expecting a pat on the back. Someone who doesn't care if anyone else knows how hard he works or how good he is at his job, because *he* knows. My editor friend Rob was a gamer. Pamela was too, and I tried to be one. Only now, when Dad was in his sixties, did I realize that my idea of who and what to admire—and why—came from him. Even in his years of eclipse, he'd been in my head.

By 1990, we were talking on the phone almost every night. Nine p.m. in California, midnight in Indy. "The Dad Report," we called those talks. We never discussed politics, religion, or our health. We talked about fantasy league tactics, trade rumors, pitching matchups, injuries, who was a gamer and who was a jake—his term for a prima donna in spikes. We talked about when to play the infield in, when to steal, the lost art of the squeeze, the tactical difference between a suicide squeeze and a safety squeeze, the moral difference between a brushback pitch, which is a pitcher's prerogative, and a beanball, which is assault.

Dad couldn't stand beanballs. "I never threw one," he said. A decent fastball reaches the plate in four-tenths of a second, giving the batter about two-tenths to track the ball's path and spin. Since the human eye takes 0.2 to 0.25 seconds to blink, the batter has a literal blink of an eye to decide to swing, check his swing, or duck. Dad thought it was a miracle that only one man had been killed on the field. In 1920, the Yankees' Carl Mays hit Cleveland shortstop Ray Chapman with a submarine pitch. It was probably a spit-ball, legal in those days. Chapman froze. The ball caromed off his head (protected only by a felt cap, as in Dad's playing days) with such force that the Yankees infielders thought he'd hit a grounder. They threw the ball around the horn while Chapman lay twitching by the plate. After a minute he stood, blood dripping from his ear, and walked to the dugout with Indians manager Tris Speaker. Twelve hours later, Chapman was dead. Despite modern helmets, Dad thought it was only a matter of time until another batter died. He loathed headhunters like Nolan Ryan and Roger Clemens. "There's a way to push a guy off the plate," he said. "Hit him on the butt." Dad said any pitcher who beans a batter should be ejected, even if he didn't mean it. "Bad control's as bad as bad intentions. The hitter's face doesn't care." He generally sided with pitchers, but liked batters who were game enough to dig in against Ryan and Clemens.

He had plenty of other opinions. Modern ballplayers were better than his generation, he said. Bigger, stronger, faster. And fundamentally worse. Why? A few got rushed to the majors, but Dad thought the problem had more to do with minor-league coaching. All you had to do was read *The Sporting News*, he said, to see who got hired as batting and pitching coaches in the minors. In his day, many of those jobs went to former major-league stars. By the 1990s, salaries were so high that former big leaguers were set for life. They weren't going to coach in Peoria for $12,000 a year. "So who are your minor-league coaches? Guys who never made it." He compared them to medical students who flunked out of med school. No wonder players reached the majors with no clue how to lay down a bunt. Dad could barely watch when a rookie jabbed his bat at the ball instead of squaring up and letting it kiss the barrel. He applauded bunters who knew the advanced art of pulling the bat backward slightly at impact to make a bunt die when it hit the infield grass.

It drove him nuts to see a team squander a hard-won advantage—particularly if he'd bet on that team. How often did the offense get a pitcher on the ropes, only to help him? Three walks load the bases in a tie game, and what happens? Some selfish, stats-minded sonofabitch hits the next pitch into a double play. "He should sit for a week," Dad said. But it never happened. Economics again: Is a manager making $100,000 going to show up a million-dollar player?

Dad liked the save, a pitcher-friendly stat that came in for its share of ridicule. The trouble with the save wasn't that it sometimes rewarded a guy who gave up two runs, because no stat is perfect. Pitchers' won-lost records reward starters on winning teams. Batting average rewards bad hops. Saves worked—the best relief pitchers tended to get the most saves. The trouble with saves was that managers made pitching changes based on the stat. It drove Dad crazy when a manager saved his best reliever for the ninth inning, even if a game's pivotal moment came in the seventh, risking a win for a chance to get his closer a save. Were managers now working for players' agents?

He thought kids should get to stay home from school on Opening Day. During my boyhood, the Reds, as the first professional team, opened the season before any other team (one of many traditions Major League Baseball ditched in the Selig era)—and he let me stay home to watch the Big Red Machine. "It's the national pastime. They play the national anthem. It's a national holiday in our house," he said.

He used to say that the older you get, the smarter your dad gets. True enough in my case. The older I got, the more I accepted his view of the game and saw how his view had shaped mine in the first place. He couldn't stand jakes, the opposite of gamers, loafing after fly balls, looking bored, standing at the plate admiring their homers, or taking a day off when the other team starts its ace. (A common excuse is "flu-like symptoms," longtime baseball code for a hangover.) Never didactic—he was the opposite of pushy—he passed along the values that were and are most central to me. Try hard. Don't complain. Be a good teammate. Win with grace, lose with more grace, and enjoy the game.

Some ballplayers are field generals, barking orders. Dad turned out to be the other kind of leader, the kind that leads by example.

LIKE MANY PRO ATHLETES, he never really understood fandom, the vicarious enjoyment of other men's games. Without a bet, who cared if the Cubs beat the Reds? Jerry Seinfeld called fandom "rooting for laundry"—cheering players who happen to be wearing your favorite team's uniform. Many pro ballplayers will check in on a TV game to see how friends or former teammates are doing, or maybe spot a pitcher's tendencies, but sitting through a game would bore them. Thanks to techies employed by their teams, they now watch games in streamlined form, with all the dead time spliced out, during video study. They can cue up particular at-bats or watch a whole game in fifteen minutes. Dad would have liked that when he was a player. He said it made more sense than the scouting reports of the past, which often amounted to "Don't give this guy anything to hit."

We talked about how the game favors gamers in the long run, a factor he called fairness and I thought of as karma. Work your butt off, never gripe, and in the long run you'll come out ahead. Or if you don't, at least you won't look back and kick yourself, because you gave your all. That's when it dawned on me that talking about baseball was our way of talking about everything. We might spend an hour on the phone, or five minutes. It didn't matter. As in baseball, it was consistency that counted. He knew the phone beside the ashtray in his smoky den would ring around midnight. He knew who was calling.

"Two homers by Héctor Villanueva—"

"Good for the Cubs," he said. "Bad for the under."

Dad liked hearing about my baseball travels— not the games as much as the screwy details: Pirates manager Jim Leyland, who was trying to quit smoking, sneaking cigs in the clubhouse tunnel; the Dodgers' Tommy Lasorda inventing new combinations of four-letter words; Reds owner Marge Schott saving dimes by charging her players for their newspapers on the road; Giants slugger Kevin Mitchell fighting off colds by eating Vicks VapoRub; Expos closer John Wetteland staying alert by munching coffee crystals out of the jar; the Padres' Chris "Tin Man" Brown skipping a game with a strained eyelid ("I slept on it wrong"); the Braves' John Smoltz burning his chest by ironing a shirt he was wearing.

Most of all, he liked tips for his fantasy team. "What else?" he'd say. "The Dads have a draft coming up."

"Hideo Nomo," I said in March 1995.

"Who?"

"Dodgers pitcher. *N-o-m-o*. Draft him."

Looking back, I think that was yet another way of saying "I love you" without coming right out and saying it.

As he aged, Dad grew sentimental about baseball for the first time. He reminisced about the pleasure of stretching your legs after a seven-hour bus ride, and the pretty girls in baseball towns, and the art of flipping a curve under a power hitter's hands to set him up for a screwball, and the cat-and-mouse game of showing a base runner a slow, obvious move to first base before picking him off with your best move.

He turned seventy in 1995. He was slowing down and starting to forget things. Leaving the stove on all afternoon, letting bathwater run until the bathroom flooded. "Losing my fastball a little," he said. He worried that he was coming down with what one of his Indy East League cronies called Olds-timers Disease.

One night when I was in Indianapolis working on a basketball story, we sat in his car in the driveway, listening to a Reds game. With Joe Nuxhall and Marty Brennaman mumbling on the radio, Dad talked about dying. It was funny, he said, but he wasn't scared of dying. He was scared of going downhill even more. His fastball gone, he didn't want to "lose my changeup, too."

What bothered him more than dying, he said, was all the baseball he would miss. He wished he could keep up with the game that had been in his blood since he first took the mound on a dusty field in 1930s Indiana. To follow the rhythm of every season—who's hot, who's hurt, how the pennant races turn out. He hoped to stick around long enough to see if the Cubs or Red Sox could win a World Series.

He didn't believe in heaven, he said, "but I think we've got spirits." Raised Baptist but never a churchgoer, he didn't mean souls as much as something simpler that might outlive us. "Not just people. Animals, too," he said. He'd grown up milking cows, slaughtering chickens and hogs. He understood the fragile hold all creatures have on life. When I was nine or ten, one of our dogs caught a squirrel and mangled it before leaving it squirming in the backyard. Dad gave me a baseball bat and told me to put the squirrel out of its misery. I struck and missed it again and again, crying and grazing the squirrel until Dad took the bat from me and finished the job.

More than twenty years later, we were talking on the phone, discussing some pitching matchup, when he mentioned that day with the squirrel. He remembered how he felt that day. He was hoping to teach me one of those life lessons fathers are supposed to teach their sons. Something about hard choices, or how something that feels wrong can be the right thing to do, or some such idea. "But you weren't old enough." The phone line went quiet for a second. "I shouldn't have put you through that," he said. "I'm sorry."

It was getting late. We said goodnight and promised to talk again tomorrow.

10

★ *Giants with Grudges* ★

BOBBY AND BARRY BONDS

Great swing, bad face."

That was Dad's take on Barry Bonds. We both admired Bonds's swing—his balanced, leonine weight shift, the lash of his black maple bat. Dad hated the way Bonds stood at the plate admiring his home runs, or rolled his eyes if an ump missed a strike call. I liked him for some of the same reasons. "It shows he cares," I said.

Dad's problem with the game's best young slugger wasn't just stylistic. To him, Bonds's theatrics suggested an uneven keel. That's what he meant by "bad face." Dad said he'd never last. Bonds might have a great season or two, he said, but would never sustain his MVP-level brilliance because "You can't get too high or too low in this game."

Then Bonds won his second MVP award.

Dad phoned me that night. "Call Hef," he said. "Tell him you should do one of those *Playboy* talks with Barry."

But Hugh Hefner didn't like sports. Hef saw politicians, jazz musicians, and movie stars as true celebrities, with athletes and TV actors a step or two below. I'd pitched Bonds to *Playboy* before and been turned down, until the spring of '93, when the politicians and celebrities on Hef's short list all fell through and it was Bonds or Dan Aykroyd.

I got in touch with Dennis "Go-Go" Gilbert, Bonds's agent, who put me off for weeks. Then Gilbert called one afternoon to say I could meet Barry the following day, after a spring-training game in Scottsdale.

"Tomorrow?" I was hoping I'd heard him wrong. Pamela was pregnant. An early test had returned a troubling result. She was scheduled for an amniocentesis the next day, and I wanted to be with her.

"Tomorrow," Gilbert said, adding, "Barry doesn't do much press. He doesn't need it." Click. Dial tone.

Dad said I should tell Go-Go to stick it. But with our first baby on the way, Pamela and I needed the money. The *Playboy* Interview paid twice as much as a typical magazine story. "You should go," she said. "Call me. And think about baby names."

I'D MET BONDS BEFORE. We'd had a few locker-room chats when he was a spindly Pirates rookie. In a 1987 story, I called him "The Sledgehammer Kid," warning fans to keep an eye out for Bobby

Bonds's son. In the accompanying photo, Barry posed with a sledgehammer he swung to build his muscles. He was all-natural in those days, six foot one, 185 pounds. After a storied college career, he'd blown through the minor leagues in only 115 games, but he wasn't a star yet. The twenty-two-year-old Bonds batted .223 in his first year in the big leagues, with 16 home runs, and finished sixth in the voting for Rookie of the Year. Still, he exuded a casual brilliance. During batting practice, the ball came off his bat with a sound few hitters produce. He could choke up on the bat and still hit a ball 450 feet. This was a rookie to keep an eye on.

When I asked about hitting, he stared into the distance over my shoulder, looking bored. So I tried music, TV, movies . . . and it turned out that he was a movie buff. He was crazy about *White Nights*, a 1985 Cold War thriller starring Mikhail Baryshnikov and Gregory Hines.

"Great dancers," I said. "Dumb movie."

"Wrong!" Bonds said, but he was smiling.

Six years and a pair of MVP trophies later, he agreed to resume our conversation. By then, Barry Bonds was more than a three-time All-Star, four-time Gold Glove winner, and the highest-paid player in Giants history ($43.75 million over six years). He was the Franchise, one of *People* magazine's Most Beautiful People, just entering his prime at the age of twenty-nine.

I met him in the Giants' spring-training clubhouse at Scottsdale Stadium, a 12,000-seat bandbox where fans mobbed Bonds before and after spring games while All-Stars Matt Williams and Rod Beck walked past unnoticed. Our interview was scheduled for that afternoon, but he gave me the slip.

Next day, same thing.

"Barry, I'm the guy from *Playboy* . . ."

"Sorry, dude. I'm busy." And he was gone.

I was left with a clubhouse full of ballplayers I didn't need to talk to. If I'd been writing a Bonds profile, I could have gathered quotes from Williams, Beck, and other Giants. (And the clubhouse attendants—nothing tells you much more about a player's character than how he treats and tips the clubbies.) But a Q-and-A is different. You need time with the subject himself.

I spent a few minutes with Dusty Baker, the Giants' manager, who said baseball was "easier for Barry" than for "regular guys." Baker, round-faced and watchful, his six-foot, two-inch frame filling out around a belly that tested the buttons on his jersey, knew the difference between All-Stars and superstars. A two-time All-Star who slugged 30 homers for the 1977 Dodgers, Baker was on deck in '74 when his Atlanta teammate Hank Aaron broke Babe Ruth's career home-run record. He was also credited with inventing the high-five. (No fooling—look it up.) When I asked about

Bonds, he said that part of his managerial style was "to cut Barry some slack. Because for guys like him, some of the hardest stuff in the world comes easy. Like hitting. But everything else gets worse. Like just getting from the parking lot to the clubhouse." Baker told me about watching Bonds sign autographs for an hour, "then he'd say he had to get going. There were still people waiting, and they got mad. This kid reached up and hit Barry in the face with a pen. Tried to hit his eye! Now, if that happened to you, how many autographs would you sign?"

I found Bobby Bonds in a corner of the clubhouse, smoking a cigarette, doing a crossword. Born in 1946, Barry's father came up at a time when black players sat on the team bus while their white teammates ate in road-trip restaurants. A right-handed hitter like his idol Willie Mays, Bobby had a sprinter's speed and upper-deck power. In 1968, he joined Mays in the Giants' outfield—the aging Willie, who as a teenager had played center for the Negro Leagues' Birmingham Black Barons while Art "Lefty" Cook pitched on the same field for the all-white Barons. Bobby Bonds clouted 39 homers in 1973 and practically invented the 30/30 club, hitting 30 or more homers and swiping 30 or more bases in the same season five times (Mays only did it twice). But he also struck out at a prodigious pace, setting the all-time mark of 189 whiffs in 1970, a record that stood for a quarter of a century.

He also held out for better pay, wore his hair in an Afro, and rolled his eyes at dumb questions from reporters. As a result, he gained a reputation for being "difficult" or even "militant," which was sportswriter code for uncooperative and black. He got traded so often—to the Yankees, Angels, White Sox, Rangers, and Indians—that a line in Terry Cashman's 1981 song "Talkin' Baseball" goes, ". . . and Bobby Bonds can play for everyone." Finally, the Rangers sold him to the Cubs. He retired in '82, eleven years before I interrupted his crossword in Scottsdale.

"Bobby, got a minute? I'm interviewing Barry. Or trying to."

The elder Bonds studied the lit end of his cigarette. "Guys always coming around asking about Barry," he said. "What do you know about him? Anything?"

"He likes movies. Nikolai, your grandson—he's named for the Baryshnikov guy in *White Nights*."

Bobby nodded. I bummed a smoke and we talked about family.

Bobby Lee Bonds came from Riverside, California, a flat Inland Empire town, home to citrus groves, segregated schools, and Ku Klux Klan meetings. Bobby and his sister Rosie first distinguished themselves on the track at Riverside Polytechnic High School. Rosie went on to set the U.S. record in the women's 80-meter hurdles.

Their parents couldn't afford a plane ticket to New York for the 1964 Olympic trials, but Ray Charles heard about Rosie's plight and gave her a cross-country ride in his private plane. Unable to pay for a hotel room on the night before the trials, she slept in Downing Stadium, made the team, and led the Olympic final in Tokyo until she peeked over her shoulder, stumbled on the final hurdle, and finished last. Years later, when her nephew Barry began stealing 30-plus bases a year, Bobby reminded him that he was only "the third-fastest person in the family. I'm faster than you, and your aunt Rosie can beat you too."

Bobby ran a 100-yard dash in 9.5 seconds and long-jumped a record twenty-five feet, three inches at Riverside Poly, where he also starred in basketball (38 points in one game), football, and baseball, gaining his first measure of fame as 1964's California High School Athlete of the Year. That was the year he signed with the Giants. Four summers later, after half a season in which he batted .370 at Triple-A Phoenix, Bobby Bonds made his major-league debut. In his first at-bat, he hit a grand slam.

At the time, his son Barry was three years old.

"I was already thinking of Barry as a ballplayer," Bobby told me. "Back when he was a baby, I'd hand him a bottle to see which hand he'd use. I wanted him to be right-handed. Not because I was and Willie was, but because being left-handed limits your positions. You can't catch or play first base. So I'd take the baby bottle out of Barry's left hand and put it in his right. But he kept switching it back, so I lost that one."

Bobby stubbed out a smoke. He was dressed and ready to go. I asked him to remind Barry that I needed some time, and he said he would. "But no promises."

That night, for what must have been the tenth time, I looked over my Bonds file.

Barry had starred at a private high school in San Carlos, California, where the baseball coach swooned over the scrawny sixteen-year-old's near-perfect balance at the plate and a swing that was "snap-your-fingers quick." The Giants selected Barry in the second round of the 1982 amateur draft, offering a $75,000 signing bonus. He was tempted, but his father and godfather— Bobby and Mays, both former Giants—told him it wasn't enough. Barry went to Arizona State, where coach Jim Brock called him the best player in school history, a history that included Sal Bando, Bob Horner, and Bobby's second cousin Reggie Jackson. Brock also called him "the worst teammate." Barry used to park his shiny black Trans-Am in Coach Brock's parking space. "He bragged about the bonus money he'd turned down, and popped off about his dad," Brock said, calling his best-ever player "rude, inconsiderate, and self-centered. I don't think he ever figured out how to get people to like him."

The pattern repeated in Pittsburgh, where sportswriters dubbed him "the Pirates' MDP: Most Despised Player." All-star outfielder Andy Van Slyke said Barry would be a superstar "if he learns to apply himself. He needs to work at it." Bonds dismissed Van Slyke as the team's "great white hope" and blew off reporters who asked follow-up questions about their feud. "My job isn't to walk in the locker room and kiss butt," he said.

Pirates manager Jim Leyland liked Barry Bonds, maybe even loved him—not only for the Hall of Fame talent he brought to the team, but for the thoughtful, vulnerable side Bonds revealed from time to time. "He tries to be a regular guy," Leyland said. "Barry would like to be liked."

He lacked the knack. Try as he might to be nice when the mood struck him, Bonds could be such an ass that even the low-key Leyland blew up at him from time to time. After one of Barry's hissy fits, the Pirates manager threw one of his own. "I've kissed your butt for three years! If you don't want to be here, get your butt off the field!" he shouted at his left fielder, who soon apologized, swearing he loved Leyland. Still, Bonds was wearing out his welcome in Pittsburgh. His split with the Pirates would be largely financial—he was getting too good and therefore too expensive for small-market Pittsburgh—but in Bonds's mind it was racial, too. He and his father both believed that the team's front office and nearly all-white press corps hoped to run him out of town. That spring, Bobby had warned his son to watch out for an ambush. A week later, when Leyland confronted Barry with a local TV crew conveniently posted nearby, the Bondses were convinced that the Pirates had staged the incident.

"It wasn't an accident. They set me up," Barry said later. As usual, he had a point. Would the same thing have happened to Andy Van Slyke? Maybe not, but Bonds lost the high ground by sticking his cleated foot in his mouth with a thoughtless quote: "I felt raped, almost. I knew how a woman who was raped felt."

In 1992, he spurned Pittsburgh's $25 million offer in favor of a six-year, $43.75 million dollar deal with the Giants. Bobby and Willie's old team.

One of Barry's first memories was of a home game at Candlestick Park in 1970, when he was five. The Reds' Bobby Tolan ripped a ball over the wall. Center fielder Mays and right fielder Bobby Bonds both leaped, getting their legs tangled as they reached over the fence. Kindergartner Barry, watching from a front-row seat, burst into tears as his father and godfather fell in a pile on the warning track. Mays lay flat on his back, Bobby beside him. At last Bobby staggered to his feet. He reached down, picked the ball from Mays's glove, and held it up for the cheering crowd to see. Mays gave the fans a woozy wave—side retired.

Bobby might have had a less bouncy path if he'd been friendlier to the press. In his day, newspaper writers still played a pivotal role in players' lives. They served as PR men for major-league teams, keeping the players' ugly secrets to themselves. The tradition dated back more than half a century to a time when team owners paid for sportswriters' travel in first-class rail cars, treating them to steak and lobster dinners while the players ate sandwiches. In return, baseball scribes portrayed skirt-chasing drunks from the young Babe Ruth to Mickey Mantle as heroes on and off the field. They lionized bigots like Ty Cobb and cheaters like spitballer Gaylord Perry, headhunters from Sal "The Barber" Maglie to Don Drysdale and Nolan Ryan. The all-white press corps, which voted on the leagues' annual MVP and Cy Young awards and decided who made the Hall of Fame, often showed less love to black players. Mays was popular, but not like Mantle. Bobby was dogged his whole career by rumors that he drank like Babe Ruth and chased almost as many skirts. Even if the rumors were true, why was Ruth beloved while Bobby Bonds was vilified? Bobby wondered why reporters adored his prickly 1975 Yankees teammate Thurman Munson while Bobby, who hit 32 homers that year to Munson's 12, was tarred as "sullen" and "surly" and quickly traded to the California Angels. Maybe the writers identified more with players like Munson, Van Slyke, Kirk Gibson, and Lenny Dykstra, who reminded them of themselves. White stars were "tough," "gutty," "gritty," and "scrappy," but black players were never called "scrappy." They were "natural athletes."

Bobby thought he was scrappy. He battled the pitcher every at-bat and suspected that the same writers who called him a disappointment, given his "natural gifts," might want to shine his shoes if he looked like Mickey Mantle. He avoided the writers when he could, kept his answers short when he couldn't.

His son came up in a different era. By the time Barry reached the majors in 1986, newspapers were losing their grip on the game. *SportsCenter* mattered more than the *Pittsburgh Post-Gazette* or *San Francisco Chronicle*. By 1993, when I caught up with him in Arizona, Barry could ignore the reporters crowding his locker—actually two lockers, per his demand. By then, he ruled his own corner of the Giants' clubhouse, with his own massage chair, sound system, and widescreen TV. He owed the writers nothing. (Even so, he claimed to have a spy in the press box, a friend who relayed negative comments the writers made about him.) Barry Bonds didn't need sportswriters because was a new sort of baseball hero. He was a TV star.

• • •

A WEEK AFTER MY LOCKER-ROOM CHAT with Bobby, Barry met me at Bear Creek Country Club near San Diego, where he was building a house. He pulled up in a spotless white Mercedes. Barry's smile was pearlier than his father's. Bobby had a gap in his front teeth, while Barry's teeth were perfect. Bobby was strong and graceful, but not handsome like Barry, who wore a mammoth diamond ring on his left hand, a diamond cross hanging from one ear, and a pendant around his neck inscribed BARRY BONDS 30/50 in diamonds and gold, commemorating his 30-homer, 50-steal season in 1990, the second such season in major-league history.

"My dad likes you," he said as a greeting. "You hungry?"

Over lunch in the clubhouse, he did a pretty good Stevie Wonder impression, singing a few bars of "Superstition," and split his appetizer with me, then pointed at the microcassette recorder I placed on the table between us.

"You writer guys. You think your job's hard," he said. "But you know what? I could learn to press 'Record' on a tape recorder and write for a newspaper or a magazine. But could you ever be good at baseball? Probably not. So don't degrade what I do, because I could put you to zero." Ben McGrath of *The New Yorker* would quote that line from my interview as evidence of Bonds's ego. What McGrath didn't see was Bonds's expression as he said it. It wasn't haughty or hostile, just watchful. He was looking for a reaction. Like his dad, he wanted to test you, to give you a poke in the chest before he'd talk.

And he had a point. He could learn to do my job, but I couldn't do his. I asked how it felt when he hit a home run.

He smiled. "Like one perfect boom. You don't hear anything, you don't even feel it hit your bat. That's the zone—everything's perfect in that one second. It's strange, it's fun, but it's only temporary."

"You often stand at the plate, admiring your homers. Are you a hot dog?"

"The way I see it, out of 600 at-bats, you might hit 30 home runs. Enjoy them!"

"Pitchers don't like it when you show them up."

"I mean no harm. That's just what makes Barry tick. It's like when I tap my glove on my chest before I catch a fly ball. People like that, but there's a point to it, too. It lets my teammates and the fans know everything's under control. You can yell, 'Mine, I got it,' but if the crowd's too loud, the other outfielder can't hear you. When I'm tapping my chest to say it's mine, you can't miss my gesture. It's like I'm moonwalking across the field."

Bonds cast himself as a pop-culture star—a specifically black star. "When I run my mouth," he said, "I'm Richard Pryor. Or I can feel smart and want everybody to listen to me, like Bill Cosby. When I signed with the Giants, everybody asked how it felt to come home, to be with my father and my idol Willie Mays—he's my godfather—and I got all choked up and I thought, 'Yes, now I'm crying like Diana Ross!'"

After lunch, we headed out to the golf course. Bonds teed up a Titleist and knocked it out of sight. The ball took a curving arc toward Riverside County. He took a mulligan. As a golfer, the Giants' $44 million man was a ten-handicapper like me. Unlike me, he whacked the occasional 320-yard drive down the middle, posing to admire it while his diamond jewelry glinted in the sun. He laughed when I hit one out of bounds.

He was a wizard at bunker shots. He opened the face of his sand wedge and swung hard, sliding the club into the sand under the ball, spraying sand on the green while his ball stopped a foot from the flag. Hitting an explosion shot from the sand, Bonds said, was a lot like hitting big-league pitching. Both called for "strength, finesse, and smartness."

Between shots, he reminisced about his brief minor-league stints in Prince William, Virginia, and Honolulu, sharing an apartment with three or four roomies, sleeping in a lounge chair and loving it because he was *a pro ballplayer*. He remembered facing his dad's old teammate

Nolan Ryan during his first big-league spring training, ducking away from Ryan's killer fastball. "I might have stepped in the bucket a little." He faced the forty-year-old Ryan three times that day and struck out on nine fastballs. "One-two-three. One-two-three. One-two-three. I was in awe." Despite his rep for surliness, Bonds sounded wistful as he recalled the frustrating process of learning to hit big-league pitching. As a rookie, he'd batted .223. In the next two seasons, he lifted his average sixty points, but in 1989, his fourth season, he fell back to .248. Leyland sat in the dugout that August and September, steaming, while his leadoff hitter swung for the fences. "The only reason he hit .248," Leyland said, "is that he spent a month and a half trying to hit his 20th home run." Bonds finished the season with 19 homers.

Still, he was learning. Learning to "see things faster," as he described the focus a hitter needs in the batter's box. He told me about a hitting drill he employed to sharpen his vision. Using a Sharpie, he'd write numbers on tennis balls, then have a batting-practice pitcher try to fire them past him. Bonds tried to read the numbers in flight. As often as not, he would rip one over the infield and say, correctly, "Six!" He learned to recognize a slider by the way the stitches on the spinning ball seem to make a red dot on the incoming pitch. He learned to see a pitch that looked cap-high as it left the pitcher's hand as "a curveball, obviously, or he wouldn't start it up there." In 1991, his fifth year with the Pirates, Bonds batted .301 with 33 homers, 114 RBIs, and 52 steals to claim his first MVP award. By then, he and Bobby had 472 major-league home runs and 678 steals, far more than any other father-son duo in baseball history. And Barry was just getting started.

Raised in San Carlos, California, an affluent, mostly white bedroom community near San Francisco, Barry Bonds grew up in a house his father bought with a loan from Willie Mays. Mays donated furniture, too, and if you believe family lore, Willie helped Bobby make a few mortgage payments by purposely losing a few big-money hands of clubhouse poker. He wanted Bobby's family to make the leap from segregated Riverside to San Carlos comfort. To men of Bobby Bonds's and Willie Mays's generation, that was success.

Barry claimed to be less touchy about race than his father and Mays. "Racism sucks, but I'd play for the Reds. I'd play for Marge." Cincinnati Reds owner Marge Schott was in the news that year for collecting Nazi memorabilia and reportedly referring to her black players as "million-dollar niggers." He said he was cool with that. "Marge could call me nigger all day. I'd just call her a white-trash trailer-park bitch while I'm cashing her checks."

Barry had attended private Junipero Serra High, an all-male Catholic school where he was one of a handful of black students. One day, he stormed home after other kids called him a nigger. When his father asked what was wrong, he said, "I hate white people!" Bobby sent him back outside and locked the front door. Barry sat on the porch for an hour before his father let him back in. There was no point in hating bigots, Bobby said. There were too many of them.

Bobby told his son about Jackie Robinson. What ballplayer ever took more shit than Jackie? This was a common refrain among baseball men of Bobby's generation. "My dad was the same way," Dusty Baker told me. "That's what our fathers always said about racial stuff. We were supposed to ask ourselves, 'What would Jackie do?' That meant a lot to me. I got in fights, I stood up for myself, but I tried to remember what my dad said, too. 'Turn the other cheek.' I tried, but that wasn't really Bobby's style. Or Barry's."

Lining up a three-foot putt, Barry took his stance over the ball, glanced at the hole, then closed his eyes.

"You putt with your eyes shut?" I asked.

"Just the short ones." He explained that, when he was younger, his father psyched him out during their golf matches by dancing around the hole, saying, "Don't choke, Barry! Don't miss it!" Barry learned to block him out by shutting his eyes.

"We're friends now," he said, "but as a kid, I never liked my dad. He never came to my Little League games. He was on the road. My mom would write 'From Dad' on my birthday presents, but he had no idea." And then there were the expectations his lineage put on him. "People always said, 'Oh, it's *easy* for Barry. He's got a *famous father* making it *easy,*" Bonds said, mimicking the haters. "Well, actually, no. My father never taught me. I hit .500 in high school, and what bat did he ever swing for me?"

In fact, Bobby attended some of his son's Little League games. He didn't want to make a scene, so he watched from his car, like Art Cook, to avoid putting pressure on his son. According to Dusty Baker, "Bobby cared more than he let on."

Barry remembered being a teenager, playing pool with his father. Loser did push-ups. Barry always lost. When he got older and started winning, Bobby quit playing pool with him.

Barry remembered spankings when he was a grade schooler. Nothing fierce—not like the belt-lashings Bobby and Dusty Baker got from their fathers. "It hurt my feelings more than anything else. But if you didn't cry, it was like you were showing him up. And don't cry too much, either. He knew it didn't hurt that bad. Just cry and apologize, and he was cool."

"You had to cry *correctly?*" I asked.

Barry nodded. "You had to know how to cry."

251

He remembered fishing trips with his father. Barry hated them. He got seasick. "I was a mama's boy. I'd rather watch my mom put her makeup on. I'd rather put on a wig and dance; we'd both pretend we were Janet Jackson. She'd say, 'Go with your father.' I always bitched that I never got to see him, then he'd plan some father-son thing and I'd be whining, 'Mom, I'm not going.'"

Bonds told me he might have been unfair to his dad. "I think I devalued a lot of the good things he tried to do." For one thing, Bobby had seen his son swinging for the fences early in his career. He pulled Barry aside and said, "Don't try to what I did. I was a home-run hitter. You can be the best all-around player *ever*." Yet, moments after telling that story, Barry went back on the attack. He called his father a limited player, saying that he couldn't imagine racking up strikeouts the way Bobby had, because striking out was "embarrassing." This was despite the fact that Bobby retired with 332 major-league home runs, while Barry currently had 176. I was starting to think of baseball's best hitter as one of the more conflicted athletes I'd ever met.

When we finished our round of golf, Susann "Sun" Bonds, Barry's wife, a petite brunette from Sweden, met us at the course. Bonds flipped me his keys. "You can drive my car," he said. I climbed into Barry's white Mercedes and followed Sun's red Porsche to their 12,000-square-foot mansion on 1.3 desert acres in Murrieta, where I almost sideswiped a boulder by the mailbox.

"Don't wreck my car, dude!" he called out the window.

Casa Bonds, still under construction, held a kitchen with a juice bar and a restaurant-quality pizza oven, a gym, a sauna, and a swimming pool with a waterfall. The chandeliered foyer featured a pair of stained-glass windows—one shaped like the sun, in honor of Sun Bonds, and the other shaped like a baseball diamond. Barry boasted that painting his house had required so many gallons of a custom-mixed shade of tan that Sherwin-Williams named the shade Bonds 103.

In the kitchen, I told Sun about my wife's amniocentesis—we'd gotten good news, all clear on the latest lab tests and ultrasound. Sun said that, with a baby on the way, I should practice "daddy duties" and handed me a spoon so I could help feed three-year-old Nikolai his Cheerios.

Bonds shook a finger at us. "You all are spoiling him!"

Barry wasn't spoiled like that, he said. One day, his parents caught him smoking a cigarette. "They made me smoke a whole pack right in front of them. It worked pretty well. I got sick, and then I didn't touch those things for a long time." He picked up his baby daughter, Shikari, and led the way outside.

We continued our talk by the pool. Bonds stretched his legs and settled into a lounge chair. Reflecting on the life he'd lived as a big-league bachelor, he recalled long, buzzy nights of "running the streets. Fame, girls, everything. One big party." But that life wore him down. He drank, smoked, never seemed to sleep. By his fourth year with the Pirates, he noticed that his lifestyle was catching up with him. He was fouling off pitches he should have driven. So he cut down on his vices. "I was in the major leagues four years before I woke up—you have to outgrow that shit," he said. He began turning down late-night invitations. He hired a nutritionist. Then he married Sun and became a baseball dad.

Bonds was twenty-six when Nikolai was born, which gave him eight years more maturity than Bobby had when Barry was born. "You think back to all the times they said, 'Wait till you have kids of your own.' All the things you said you'd never do—you'd never spank your kids, or yell at them. Yeah, right. It's fun, because now you know you were sticking your foot in your mouth when you were little. You start giving your own parents the benefit of the doubt."

Some of my questions touched the usual bases. On being misunderstood: "The worst is when people say we don't try. I don't think there's one major-league player who doesn't try. It's *embarrassing* to drop a fly ball. It's *embarrassing* to strike out. But say what you want. I don't need your sympathy." On racism: "My grandfather grew up in a time when black people had to walk on the other side of the street, and he was never angry about it. That seemed weird to me. When he talked about some guy calling him boy or nigger, I'd say, 'Man, I would have killed him.' But my grandfather said, 'If you were born at that time, you'd know how it was.'"

He liked curveball questions.

"Did you celebrate when *People* magazine named you one of the world's beautiful people?"

He laughed. "When you don't have money, you're ugly," he said. "When you have a little bit of money, you're cute, and when you get rich, you're fine as hell. I don't think I'm very good-looking, but now some people tell me, 'Oh, you are so fine.' I'm like, 'Give me a break.'"

"When you dream at night," I asked, "is it baseball?"

"All the time! I hit a home run, run the bases. Then I hit another one. I hit three. I hit four. Now I have a chance to break the all-time record. All of a sudden, I'm at a zoo, or on top of the Empire State Building, trying to get to the ballpark. They're trying to find me, but they go, 'Wait a minute, he's gone,' and they send up a pinch hitter."

Our interview ran in *Playboy* in July 1993, the year Bonds batted .336 and clouted 46 homers on his way to his third MVP award. It made a few ripples in the seasonal tide of baseball news. At first, Bonds denied telling me the Pirates "set me up" at spring training in '92, but I had pressed "Record" on my tape recorder, just as he would have if he'd been a reporter. Months later, before a Giants home game, he left the batting cage and walked straight to where I was standing.

"I saw you talking to my dad again," he said. "What's the matter, you don't like me anymore?" I told him I thought he might still be mad about the Pirates quote. Instead, he smiled. "Shit happens, dude."

BARRY BONDS WENT ON TO WIN four more MVP awards, giving him as many as Mays, Williams, and DiMaggio combined. And sure enough, shit happened. It had to do with that bad face of his. His uneven keel.

Dad and I never thought much of Oakland's Mark McGwire. "A big galoot," Dad called him. Unlike his "Bash Brothers" teammate José Canseco, who had Bonds-like speed to go with his power, McGwire was a limited guy, a mistake-hitter. But in 1997, he got traded to St. Louis (for T. J. Mathews) and turned into Hercules.

McGwire smacked 58 homers for the Cardinals that year while a still-slender Barry Bonds hit 40 for the Giants.

There was locker-room talk even then. What was McGwire on? It wasn't just Canseco and McGwire—in the late '90s, second-tier players like Brady Anderson and Ken Caminiti bulked up and went from 15 home runs a year to 40-plus. Soon, McGwire and the Cubs' Sammy Sosa were swatting 60-plus homers, setting the sports world on its ear, while Bonds was stuck in the 30s and 40s. Everyone knew McGwire was taking andro, a steroid precursor that was banned in the Olympics but still legal in baseball. Andro and more, some said.

One bright spring day in 2000, I sat with Canseco in the Tampa Bay Rays' dugout, inches from his Hindenburg biceps. We talked about his buddy McGwire, whose 70 homers two years before had topped the all-time record by nine. "It's incredible," I said, "to beat Ruth and Roger Maris by a month's worth of homers." Like others who covered the sport, I thought McGwire's feat was literally not credible. The Cards' slugger had gone from 22 home runs at age twenty-seven to 70 at the age of thirty-four, when he should have been over the hill.

"Incredible," I said again.

Canseco nodded. "He's a hell of a hitter." Then he put his fingers to his lips. *Shhh.*

Around that time, baseball's best player was watching McGwire, his inferior in every way—his popular *white* inferior—become the new Babe Ruth. McGwire, not Bonds, was the game's hero. Nobody seemed to care that the numbers proved Bonds was better. Through the 1998 season, McGwire had 457 career homers to Bonds's 411; McGwire also had 11 career stolen bases, zero MVP awards, and zero Gold Glove awards to Bonds' 445 steals, three MVPs, and eight Gold Gloves. Still it was McGwire whose jersey flew off souvenir stands, McGwire who drew adoring crowds to batting practice, McGwire who was TV's favorite player and *Sports Illustrated*'s Sportsman of the Year. "From his 20-inch biceps to his 500-foot blasts, everything about McGwire is Bunyanesque," *SI*'s Tom Verducci wrote, "including his heart."

That was the year Bonds batted .303 with 37 home runs, 122 RBIs, 28 steals, and another Gold Glove. But who noticed? Sosa and McGwire finished one-two in MVP voting, while Bonds came in eighth. Until then, he had worked out almost every day, but Barry Bonds was never what you'd call a gym rat. He watched what he ate. He spent the occasional hour in the gym. He supplemented his diet with protein shakes. All the while, McGwire's growing popularity ate at him. "I know how I'm perceived," the still-lean, still-clean Bonds said. "I'm supposed to be some kind of monster." Meanwhile, he saw President Bill Clinton, baseball commissioner Bud Selig, *SportsCenter* anchors, Roger Maris's family, and millions of other baseball fans hail McGwire as the game's leading man.

Though he has never come right out and admitted it, it's clear that Bonds joined the juicers during the 1998–99 off-season. Unable to beat 'em, at least in the home-run department, he apparently joined McGwire, Sosa, and dozens—if not hundreds—of other major-league players in using "the shit" to build muscle and recover from the sprains, strains, and other assorted insults a player's flesh is heir to. It's worth remembering that this was only one of the changes he made. He also switched to a state-of-the-art maple bat that was harder and denser than the ash Louisville Sluggers that generations of hitters had wielded since the days of the 36-inch, 40-ounce hickory cudgels Babe Ruth waved at enemy pitchers. (Bonds choked up on his 34-inch, 31½-ounce maple bat, making him cobra-quick at the plate.) Maple bats were perfectly legal, while anabolic steroids had been on baseball's banned-substances list since 1991. But while the NFL began testing players for steroids in 1987, and the NBA followed suit in 1999, baseball wouldn't get around to testing for steroids until 2003. Why rock the boat when the game was booming? And if you were Barry Bonds in 1998, watching an obvious juicer like McGwire make headlines and history, you had every reason to picture a simple calculation. Call it $B+MD>M$. Bonds plus McGwire's drugs is greater than McGwire.

That winter, he said goodbye to protein shakes and hello to the shit. And it worked. Bonds's home-run output went from 34 in 1999 to 49 in 2000 to 73 in 2001, the year he broke McGwire's record. Pitchers walked him a record 177 times that season. In the box seats, sitting next to her mom, ten-year-old Shikari Bonds waved a sign that read PLEASE PITCH TO DADDY. Her daddy's body looked different by then. The lean, handsome Bonds had morphed into a thick-necked, froggish fellow. Choking up on his maple bat, he turned up his nose at pitches a half inch off the black as if to sniff, "That ain't my style." But when he swung, it was so deadly quick you needed slow motion to see the sudden but balanced weight shift, the lash of the bat, and there it goes, the ball a dot in the night sky on its way to McCovey Cove. In that steroidal season, Barry Bonds was the best hitter the game had ever seen, better than Ruth, DiMaggio, Williams, Mantle, and Mays in their primes. Like Lance Armstrong at his chemically assisted peak, the best athlete with the best drugs, Bonds reached an asterisky level of performance that may never be matched.

A year later, he hit "only" 46 homers while

batting .370 with 110 RBIs in only 403 official at-bats. He was so good, it was almost like cheating. In 2004, he smacked 45 homers in a mere 373 official at-bats. He wasn't hurt, just so feared that pitchers walked him an insane 232 times, well over a third of the times he came to the plate. He was intentionally walked 120 times.

To put those numbers in perspective, consider that Babe Ruth walked 137 times in 1927, the year he hit 60 homers. Roger Maris had a career-high 94 walks in 1961, the year he hit 61. Joe DiMaggio never walked more than 80 times in a season, while eagle-eyed Ted Williams topped out at 162. Willie Mays never walked more than 112 times, and was never intentionally walked more than 20 times in a season—a hundred times fewer than Bonds in 2004, the year he fidgeted in the batter's box while other teams issued him 120 free passes.

How allergic were pitchers to pitching to Bonds? In 1998, he became the first batter in fifty-four years to be issued an intentional walk with the bases loaded: with the Diamondbacks leading the Giants 8–6 in the ninth, Arizona manager Buck Showalter ordered the intentional pass, and it worked. Arizona won the game, 8–7. By the time he retired nine years later, his reputation in tatters due to drug rumors, Bonds held a couple of other telling distinctions. Greg Maddux, the best pitcher of his generation, had intentionally walked him nine times, the most of any pitcher. Bonds had also been intentionally walked 41 times with the bases empty, more than any other hitter ever.

Enhanced by steroids, Barry Bonds fundamentally changed the pitcher-hitter dynamic. Talent plus drugs broke the game, leaving a crucial question unanswered: What if Bonds had stayed clean? How good would he have been?

Lance Armstrong, perhaps the closest parallel, isn't close enough. Armstrong, who once looked me in the eye during an interview and dared me to call him a doper, wasn't Bonds's equal in his sport. Like Bonds, he took performance-enhancing drugs to keep up with other elite athletes who were taking performance-enhancing drugs. But unlike Bonds, he couldn't beat them without joining them. There is every reason to think that Bonds, who was better than McGwire in every way but homer total even before he started doping, could have become the hero of the steroids era instead of its goat. Even clean, Bonds was a cut above everyone else.

"Ken Griffey was the greatest I played with," Bret Boone says, "but Bonds was the greatest player I've ever seen. Power, quickness, recognizing pitches—it's like he recognized pitches before the pitch was thrown. There have been some great players in our time, but Barry Bonds was at a higher level."

To me, that's what makes Bonds's story tragic in

the classic sense. A fatal flaw brought him down: out of jealousy for Mark McGwire, Barry Bonds ruined his legacy and his life.

Maybe his problem was that he learned the wrong lesson from his father. He nursed grudges like Bobby, though with less cause, and without attaining the level of grace Bobby reached late in his life, when Bobby told me, "Do you know what I'm proudest of? That now I'm known as Barry Bonds's father."

Today, looking back on the time I spent with Barry Bonds, I remember the end of our poolside talk. Bonds, at twenty-eight, was still new to the Giants. His father was the team's hitting coach. Barry said he needed no coaching from his dad. Still, he framed his last answer in family terms. When I asked if he'd changed since we first met, in his rookie year, he said yes. "I'm more emotional now," he said. "You get afraid of when baseball might end. You get older. You lose it, you get hurt. Shit happens."

I asked how he hoped to be remembered.

"I may never make the Hall of Fame," he said. "But I *want* to make the Hall of Fame, partly because of my father. Not for the status or myth. I just want my photo or my bat there, to say that this is my family and I was part of it, and part of baseball."

As it turns out, the best hitter of his time, if not of all time, may never make the Hall of Fame.

• • •

AROUND MY HOUSE, we remember Bonds for a whole 'nother reason.

While I was hanging around Scottsdale Stadium in 1993, waiting for Barry, his dad introduced me to a family friend. That night, in a phone call home, I mentioned Bobby and Barry's friend Calloway.

Pamela said, "Wait—who?"

"Just a friend of theirs."

"Calloway?" she said. "That's *it*."

And it was. Calloway Marin Cook was born four months later.

Cal Cook. Dad liked that. He said it sounded like a ballplayer's name.

11

★"My Father's Dream"★
MICHAEL JORDAN

Millions of fans remember that Michael Jordan took a time-out from basketball to try baseball, but how many remember why?

"It had to do with my father," he said.

In the fall of 1993, four months after leading the Chicago Bulls to their third consecutive NBA title—the "threepeat" that secured his standing as the basketball hero of his time, if not all time—Jordan called a press conference near his home in suburban Chicago. Word had leaked out the night before: Michael's quitting!

His teammate Scottie Pippen was watching a White Sox–Blue Jays playoff game on TV when a friend called with the news. Pippen phoned Jordan.

"Is it true?"

"It's true. I'm gone," Jordan said. They were the words Babe Ruth used more than half a century before, when his old teammate Joe Dugan came to see him on his deathbed. "Joe, I'm gone," Ruth said as both men wept. "I'm gone, Joe."

Sunglasses hid Pippen's tears during the 1993

press conference. Bulls owner Jerry Reinsdorf, introducing Jordan, said, "It's been an honor and a pleasure to have Michael here for nine years. I can only imagine what it was like seeing Babe Ruth, because I used to think—I used to say this man was the Babe Ruth of basketball. I've now come to think that Babe Ruth was the Michael Jordan of baseball."

That got a smile from the guest of honor. Over the next ten minutes, aside from a dig at sports reporters ("I've always said I'd never let you guys run me out of the game, so don't think that you've done it"), Jordan explained that he had lost his desire to win NBA titles. "I've reached the pinnacle. I've always said that when I lose that sense of motivation, that sense that I can prove something, it's time for me to leave." Like many great athletes, he was driven to prove his doubters wrong. But where were the doubters now? He had won an NCAA title for North Carolina with a last-second shot. He had won three NBA championships, three MVP trophies, the Rookie of the Year award, the Defensive Player of the Year award, and seven straight scoring titles. "It was a matter of waiting until this time, when basketball was near, to see if my heart would change. I went through all the stages of getting myself prepared for next year, but the desire was not there."

Jordan mentioned his father. "He saw my last

basketball game, and that means a lot." James Jordan, a forklift operator and handyman who moved his family from Brooklyn to Wilmington, North Carolina, when Michael was a baby, had died that summer, a month after the Bulls' three-peat. And he hadn't just died. He'd been murdered.

Driving home from a friend's funeral in Wilmington, James Jordan, aged fifty-six, pulled into a rest stop off I-95. He parked and fell asleep. A pair of carjackers spotted him snoozing in the cherry-red Lexus his son had given him, license plate UNC0023. The joyriders were planning to rob a motorist and steal his car. One of them had a .38 pistol. When James Jordan stirred, the carjacker panicked and shot him in the chest. Picking through the dead man's pockets, the shooter found his wallet and driver's license. "I believe we killed Michael Jordan's dad!" They drove south and dumped James Jordan in a creek near the border between the Carolinas, where his body was found ten days later. Meanwhile, the killers tried on a pair of NBA championship rings Michael had given his father. They called their friends on James's cell phone, which led to their capture. One of them was wearing a Michael Jordan T-shirt when he was arrested.

At the retirement press conference, Jordan referred to his dad. His father had first suggested he retire from basketball in 1990, when Michael was on his way to a fourth straight scoring title. Michael said, "No, I haven't won a champion-ship." A year later, after the Bulls' first NBA title, James brought up the subject again. Michael said, "No, I'm not finished winning."

Few fans and reporters had noticed the hints he dropped about his father. Speculation about Jordan's retirement centered on his gambling: there was talk that he had lost hundreds of thousands of dollars playing golf and casino card games, talk that the game's marquee attraction was dropping out to serve a "secret suspension," a face-saving move that would spare him and the league a season of embarrassing headlines. But the headlines never came. His gambling debts were real, but not earthshaking. The Bulls were paying him $4 million a year, a fraction of his total income from Nike and other sponsors. Like another golf gambler, Phil Mickelson, Jordan could drop a million or four without skipping one of the off-the-list thousand-dollar bottles of wine he routinely ordered at restaurants. Like my dad, he felt there was no point in betting unless a loss stung and a win changed your day. For some, that means betting ten dollars. For others, it's a hundred. But to a $40 million-a-year man like Jordan, betting $100,000 on a round of golf represented exactly what a hundred-dollar bet means to a man making $40,000 a year. Jordan bet a lot and lost a lot, but he won some bets, too. He quit basketball in October 1993, not because of his gambling debts, but for more complicated reasons.

This may be the only thing Michael Jordan and ninety-eight-year-old Julia Ruth Stevens have in common: they returned to baseball to honor their fathers.

JAMES JORDAN ALWAYS THOUGHT of his son Michael as a baseball player. James, who grew up in rural North Carolina in the 1950s, loved cars and baseball. He used to stick out his tongue when concentrating on an engine or racing around the bases. A local star, he played in "mixed" games with white players until the Ku Klux Klan broke them up.

Michael's earliest memories were of having a backyard catch with his dad. As author Roland Lazenby tells the story, the young Jordan grew up playing baseball. "One day Michael was swinging away with a bat and a block of wood with a nail in it, only to discover that the missile had struck his older sister in the head and stuck there." Well into his teen years, he was better at baseball than basketball—North Carolina's Little League Player of the Year, a fastball pitcher and slugging short-stop. When his father offered to buy him a steak if he hit a home run, Michael clouted one into the parking lot. Even after three

NBA titles, he said, "I've never experienced anything in sports like hitting one out of the park."

As a teenager, he played baseball in the local Babe Ruth League and at Wilmington's Laney High School, but was more of a standout on the hardwood. And basketball was thought to be more hospitable to black players. The game took over Michael's life, though James never saw it as his son's only goal. In the late '80s, seeing NFL stars Bo Jackson and Deion Sanders double-dip at major-league baseball, James said, "You could do that. You've got the skills." As Michael recalled later, "He thought I had proved everything I could in basketball, and I might want to give baseball a shot. We talked about baseball again and again, and he said it wasn't too late to try. And then he was killed."

Shaken by his father's murder, Jordan sought a way to maintain and even deepen their connection. As he told Bulls owner Jerry Reinsdorf, who also owned the White Sox, "It was my father's dream that I be a baseball player." In 1994, he tried living up to the dream.

That spring, I watched Jordan play for the Double-A Birmingham Barons. Willie Mays had played for the city's Black Barons in the Negro League days around the time Art Cook pitched for the Barons. Half a century later, Jordan muffed his first fly ball for the White Sox' Double-A farm club and went oh-for-three at the plate. But he got better. He looked smooth enough in the outfield that spring, gliding under a fly ball or playing a carom off the right-field fence. He wasn't so smooth at the plate, where he looked taller and thinner than he did on the basketball court, flailing at low-outside breaking balls. His front knee collapsed backward as he started his swing, making his swing look a little effeminate.

The press smelled blood. Steve Wulf of *Sports Illustrated* filed a story headed ERR JORDAN. According to Wulf, "He called the first-base umpire 'the ref.' In the field, he played a single into a double and an out into a single . . . Barely concealing their sneers, scouts and players and writers ask one another, 'Have you seen him?' They are not talking about Oddibe McDowell." *SI*'s cover read BAG IT, MICHAEL! Jordan was angry, but the ire that fueled great moments on the basketball court—no one ever held a grudge tighter than he did—was no help on the diamond. He pressed and played worse.

In April, sitting by his locker in Birmingham's Regions Park, Jordan sounded worried. "It's been embarrassing, frustrating. It can make you mad," he told the *New York Times*'s Ira Berkow. "I don't remember the last time I had all those feelings at once." He'd been trying different bats, but none felt right in his hands. He'd struck out four times in a game—the golden sombrero. "I lost confidence at the plate. I lived in a situation where I had the world at my feet. Now I'm just another minor leaguer . . ."

Owner Reinsdorf thought Jordan might be "seeking to suffer. I wonder if Michael is in some way trying to do penance for the murder of his father."

Or was he just in a slump? Or on a steep learning curve? Jordan hadn't played baseball since high school, and even then he'd been a pitcher. After thirteen years off, he was bucking monumental odds. For every two hundred high school players, one gets drafted by a major league organization. Of those elite few, only three out of a hundred will ever play an inning in the Show.

For all his troubles, Jordan had several things going for him. He was one of the best athletes in sports history, with a work ethic to match. Nobody in the Southern Association spent more time in the batting cage. Or had more motivation. "My dad's with me," he said, "wherever I go."

He improved as the season went on. On defense, "Err Jordan" became one of the better outfielders in the Southern Association—possibly the fastest, with a strong throwing arm. At the plate, he scattered enough singles to lift his batting average past .200. Through eight-hour bus rides and one-for-fifteen stretches, he spoke to his father every day—not in words, but "in the subconscious," as he put it. In the end, he stole 30 bases and drove in 51 runs, third-best on the team. He batted .202, a number often cited to prove his failure. It was actually pretty impressive for a thirty-one-year-old who was facing professional pitching for the first time—and facing any sort of pitching for the first time since he was a teenager.

Steve Wulf changed his tune. Calling his *Sports Illustrated* story "a little smarmy and a little wise-ass," Wulf wrote a follow-up later in 1994. By then, he said, Jordan "was a totally different player. He had turned himself into a baseball player. I said, 'My God, I was wrong. We were wrong.'" But *SI*, unwilling to admit its mistake, killed the follow-up.

FILMMAKER RON SHELTON, the former minor-league infielder who directed *Bull Durham, Cobb, White Men Can't Jump*, and five other movies, sympathized with Jordan. The sixty-eight-year-old Shelton remembers "grinding up the ladder one bloody notch at a time. The bus rides, the lack of days off. Bad lights and wild pitches coming straight at your head . . ." In 2010, he made an ESPN documentary recasting Jordan's minor-league sojourn as "a qualified triumph for Michael."

Shelton grew up in Santa Barbara in the 1950s, the son of a Brooklyn Dodgers fan. "We liked the Cubs and Cardinals, too, because in those days before the Dodgers and Giants moved west,

Chicago and St. Louis were the closest big-league towns, geographically." Listening to games on the radio with his dad, he soaked up the game's rhythms. "My dad loved the Cardinals' Gashouse Gang, but in our backyard games he was always the Dodgers and I was the Braves. Learning to lose was important. I threw a fit one time when I lost, and he punished me—I wasn't allowed to touch a baseball for three weeks."

After his father died, Shelton went through his possessions. He found several boxes full of envelopes. "They were letters I'd sent while I traveled the country playing minor-league baseball. I'm not sure how many fathers and sons shared as much as we did, even if we didn't talk a lot. And the main thing he taught me had nothing to do with baseball. It was about being a father. How to draw boundaries and enforce them consistently. How to disagree without arguing. How to give a son or daughter room to test themselves without parental hovering. A lot of it came down to sharing a game that rewards individual achievement in a team setting. The metaphors are obvious: boundaries, rules, and the sort of love that lasts. Most of all, it was just fun to smell fresh-cut grass and rub oil in your glove and get dirt on your pants and pretend you're Eddie Mathews or Ducky Medwick—though my father made a point of saying what we should and shouldn't learn from ballplayers. You learn how to hit a ball or play third base from your baseball heroes, but you learn about being a man from your dad."

In fact, he said, his best-known character, the catcher Kevin Costner played in *Bull Durham*, owed his grit to Shelton's father. "My dad's appreciation of those who did their jobs at a high level without recognition stuck with me. I always loved guys like Crash Davis, who never got the break he needed, but it doesn't affect the way he does his job." Quoting his dad, Shelton used a word I'd often heard from mine. "Crash is a gamer, a term that predated my father but was built into everything he believed in. You played hard and never complained and it was okay to have fun doing it. That's Crash."

Shelton's five minor-league seasons from 1967 to '71 gave him his own view of Michael Jordan's story. He hated seeing sportswriters and fans dismiss Jordan's quixotic season in the minors as a debacle, as if a typical fan or sports-writer could hit .200 against Double-A pitching. Shelton's 2010 documentary, *Jordan Rides the Bus*, was meant to erase that smear.

"Baseball had a special place in Michael's heart because it was his father's favorite sport," he told me. "His transcendent gifts were in basketball, but had he concentrated on baseball he might have been a good player, even a major leaguer."

A COUPLE YEARS AFTER JORDAN returned to the NBA, I spent a day with him for a basketball story. When we shook hands, his enveloped mine. Jordan's hands are enormous, bigger than most NBA centers' hands. His aura was regal, almost electric, like the sparkle off his diamond earring. He was mildly quotable, as usual. Like Tiger Woods, Tony La Russa, and Derek Jeter, Jordan is one of those sports figures who are smarter than their quotes. You see the intelligence playing behind their eyes while they listen to a question, consider their options, and give you the safest answer. This is the nature of modern sports journalism: the subjects don't need publicity. They have managers, agents, publicists, and Twitter ghosts for that. When they talk to the press, the idea is to say as little as possible. Shelton's Crash Davis understood the equation almost thirty years ago, when he told phenom Nuke LaLoosh to "Learn your clichés."

What surprised me was how Michael Jordan perked up when the talk turned to baseball. When I said I'd seen him play in Alabama, where my dad pitched a million years ago, Jordan smiled.

"Your dad played in Birmingham?"

We spent half an hour sitting around, talking. What he remembered most about minor-league baseball, he said, was "the camaraderie. With basketball players, when the game's over, it's *whisk, whisk, whisk,* going in ten different directions. Baseball players hang out more." Unlike his Bulls teammates, the other Barons wore jeans. "Basketball players tend to be fashion-conscious. I think that's because we're wearing shorts on the court. We want people to see us dress up." Of course, his baseball teammates were also poorer than NBA players. And younger. "A lot of times, I felt old." Succumbing to peer pressure, Old Man Mike tried chewing tobacco. It made him dizzy. On the road, he was the only one who could afford to pay extra for premium cable and movies, so other players spent their twenty-dollar per diem on the Western Steer buffet and then crowded into Michael's room, the Barons' unofficial theater.

"They'd stay up all night, drinking beer like water, then go four-for-five the next day," he said, enjoying the memory. He recalled how his teammates kept asking about his NCAA and NBA titles, and how he'd pick their brains about hitting: How fast can you read the spin on a breaking ball? Which pitchers throw particular pitches on particular counts? "The locker room and the motel room, they were classrooms for me."

After his bad tobacco buzz, he stuck to sunflower seeds. Being Jordan, he starred at dugout basketball. "That's where you spit sunflower seeds at a Gatorade cup. Basketball with seeds. It takes more than a year to get great at it, but I got pretty good. And that's the stuff you remember in baseball: the everyday nuances that fill up the time. Playing cards, checkers, dominoes, passing time in a rain delay."

After a year with the Barons, Jordan returned to the Bulls (Chicago, not Durham). From 1995 to '98, he led them to a second threepeat, and coach Phil Jackson saw a difference in him. According to Jackson, "Michael had rediscovered the joy of bonding with other men. Instead of simply glaring at his teammates and expecting them to be just like him, Michael adopted a new way of leading." He was a mellower, more tolerant leader. "A better leader."

The words *mellow* and *Michael* made for a rare pairing, but Jackson wasn't the only one to notice the difference. As Jordan told *SI*'s Jack McCallum of his time in Birmingham, "There were a lot of long nights. I'd think about my father, and how he loved baseball and always talked about it. And I knew he was up there watching me play, and it made him happy. And it made me happy, too."

As we parted, Jordan gave me a brotherly smack on the back. "The Barons. Damn," he said, smiling. "The Birmingham Barons . . ."

12
★ A Pirate's Life ★
THE DAVISES

Ron Davis was dancing in his den, reading the crawl across the bottom of his TV screen: . . . NEW YORK METS TRADE IKE DAVIS TO PITTSBURGH PIRATES FOR ZACK THORNTON AND A PLAYER TO BE NAMED . . .

The deal was no blockbuster, and no compliment to his son. Twenty-six-year-old Zack Thornton was a minor-league pitcher of no particular distinction. The trade meant that the Mets were giving up on Ike and handing the first-base job to Lucas Duda. Which was fine with Ron, who took the news like a singing cowboy. "Yee-ha! Now he'll get a chance to show what he can do."

Twenty-five hundred miles away, Ike looked shaken. Mets manager Terry Collins had called him into his office beneath the stands at Citi Field to break the news. After that brief meeting, Ike found a place to be alone. By the time he faced reporters, his eyes were watery and red. It hurts to get traded, even if it means that another club wants you, because the first thing it means is that the team whose uniform you're wearing doesn't want you. And maybe it hurts a little more when your first team lets you go. Ike had been a Met since he signed with them out of college. Tomorrow would be the fourth anniversary of his big-league debut, when he singled twice for a franchise that hoped he'd be its first baseman and cleanup hitter for the next decade, a hope he shared. "That's the tough part," he told the *New York Post*. "I made my childhood dreams come true here, playing in the big leagues. But it's just a stepping-stone."

"I keep telling Isaac I got traded three times, released three times, and sold once," Ron told me. "And while it may not be the 'correct' thing to say, there's no big difference between teams. The real difference is between the majors and the minors. Once you make the majors, it's the same hotels, same airlines, same ballparks, same money. It's just different color uniforms."

Did Ike feel the same way? "I don't know," Ron said, mindful of his son's independence. "I hope so, but I'm not speaking for him. Sometimes it's hard to tell what he's thinking."

Later, when I caught up with Ike, he said getting traded had stung until he got used to the idea. "Now I want to put on a Pirate uniform." As for the headlines about his departure from New York, he shrugged. "Little things make big stories in New York. I had a bad season and the Mets sent me away. Now my job's to help the team that wants me."

You might think a team that trades for a player would roll out the welcome mat: help him find a place to live, chip in on moving expenses, pick him up at the airport. You'd be wrong. Before the trade, Ike and a couple of friends had been renting a Manhattan apartment in a high-rise on the Upper East Side. A Mets-fan Chevrolet dealer comped him a car. After the trade, he left his apartment keys with his roomies, who began looking for another friend to split the rent. He turned in the car and found a place in Pittsburgh where he had no immediate need for a car: a hotel next door to the Pirates' PNC Park. "I like it here." He had room service and maid service and he could walk to work.

The Pirates planned to platoon him with right-hand-hitting first baseman Gaby Sánchez. Ike still hoped to earn a full-time gig. He knew that platooning could be hazardous to his future, since the "platoon player" label tends to stick. Once a team sits a left-handed hitter against lefties, or a right-handed hitter against right-handed pitchers, it's next to impossible for the platooned player to shake the label. He doesn't get enough at-bats against same-handed pitchers to prove he can hit them, and the scarcity of those at-bats makes the job harder still: the ball starts to look strange from the scarcely seen angle, while each of those at-bats takes on added meaning. That puts a platooned player under the kind of pressure that makes sense of the old saying "Don't think, just hit."

Was Ike better off after the trade? Did it give him a new start, or make him damaged goods?

As Art Cook used to say, there's one answer to every baseball question: "It depends."

The Mets had been dividing Ike's time with Duda and right-handed-hitting Josh Satin in the team's usual confused and confusing fashion. At least platooning with the Pirates would be predictable. Ike would start against right-handed starting pitchers, giving him two-thirds of the at-bats to Gaby Sanchez's one-third. "I can make an impact here," Ike said.

Steel City's new first baseman was eager to prove himself to Pirates manager Clint Hurdle. The fifty-six-year-old Hurdle welcomed Ike to town by sitting him down and saying two things: "One, we're glad to have you. Two, you don't need to carry our ball club." The Pirates had Andrew McCutchen, the National League MVP in 2013, to do that. And Hurdle knew how hard it can be for a young hitter to live up to his rep. In 1978, after he lit up Triple-A pitching for the American Association's Omaha Royals, *Sports Illustrated* put Hurdle on the cover as THIS YEAR'S PHENOM. Injuries, a drinking problem, and the relentless rigor of big-league pitching derailed his career, and now the barrel-chested, gray-haired manager, limping on a ruined hip that would need off-season surgery, offered Ike what he'd wished for in his own playing days: "a clean chalkboard." Ike would start against every right-handed starter, batting sixth or seventh rather than cleanup, to keep expectations in check. Other than that, Hurdle would leave him alone.

Hurdle even joked about Ike's dad. As he told a reporter after the trade, he remembered facing Twins fireballer Ron Davis a quarter century ago. "That guy was tough," Hurdle said. "Threw hard. Sunk it." Told that he'd gone two-for-two in his career against Ron Davis, with three RBIs, he laughed. "Really? Don't bring that up when Ron rolls into town."

In his third game for the Pirates, with the bases loaded and Pittsburgh trailing Cincinnati 2–0, Ike faced the Reds' Mike Leake, a former teammate at Arizona State. On the first pitch, Ike planted his front foot and uncoiled his core muscles. He connected. Leake's sinker broke his bat. Still, the ball took off on a tall arc. Right fielder Jay Bruce turned and watched it clear the fence. Ike's grand slam, his first homer for the Pirates, came only two weeks after his April 5 game-winner against Cincinnati for the Mets. It made him the first big-league player to clout grand slams for two teams in the season's first month. He was the third ever to hit slams against the same opponent in the same season, a feat first accomplished by Ray Boone in 1953.

Leake tipped his cap to Ike after the game. "I broke his bat and he still hit it out. That's how strong he is," he said.

IKE LIKED HIS NEW MANAGER. He liked his new team. He liked Pittsburgh, a lower-boil town than New York, where a guy could go oh-for-eight without seeing his picture in a tabloid, Photoshopped to look like a goat. Ike Davis was a happy Pirate. Then, enigmatic as ever, he slumped. He went homerless for more than a month. He batted .173 with one home run in a month and a half. The Pirates seemed to lose faith in him. Sánchez, his right-hand-hitting platoon counterpart, got more at-bats. Soon, Ike was watching error-prone third baseman Pedro Álvarez taking grounders at first during infield practice. He saw the writing on the wall when Hurdle wrote Álvarez's name into the starting lineup posted in the Pirates' dugout—at first base. Ike was listed among the subs at the bottom of the card.

"There's no point complaining," he told me. "I'll just try to stay ready."

In August, pinch-hitting in the bottom of the eighth, he belted a three-run homer to beat the Cardinals. CBS Sports' blogger was less than impressed:

Davis isn't playing every day with Pedro Alvarez moving across the diamond, and his home run was just his second one in August.

At least that game-winner earned him a start. In the second inning of the Pirates' next game, facing Cardinals ace Adam Wainwright, Ike turned on a cut fastball.

Davis followed his heroics of Tuesday night, when he slammed a pinch-hit, three-run homer, by mashing another Wednesday afternoon to key a victory over St. Louis. The latest blast doinked off a speaker an estimated 447 feet away from home plate.

Still, he was a second-stringer. Late in August, Álvarez homered three times in three games to reaffirm his claim to the first-base job. Then, faster than you can say Daniel Day-Lewis, Álvarez hurt his left foot. His diagnosis proved as thorny as Ike's left-ankle woes in 2011: At first, the club's medical staff called it a toe sprain, a day-to-day issue. Weeks later, as Álvarez clomped around the clubhouse in a boot that immobilized his foot, he was told he had a "stress reaction." He was out for the year.

Ike empathized with Álvarez. They were

friends—teammates tend to like Ike—and he told Álvarez he didn't want ABs his friend deserved. "I want to beat you out." Even so, Ike got new life in Pittsburgh when Álvarez got the boot. When we spoke in September, Ike was starting again while the Pirates, fighting for a spot in the playoffs, won fifteen times in eighteen games. "This is fun," he told the *New York Post*. "I don't have any bad remarks about the Mets. This is just different. We didn't win many games there, or have chances to make the postseason." Playing in a pennant race changed everything, he said. "It takes away from the selfishness of the game, as far as 'What are my stats?' When a guy's on second base with no outs, I'm just thinking of getting him over to third, no matter what. If I hit a grounder to first, I'm happy. It's all about winning. That's how baseball is supposed to be played."

We texted and talked in September. Ike and the Pirates were in the thick of a playoff race, four and a half games behind the Cardinals in the National League's Central Division, vying with four other teams for wild-card spots.

"A couple years ago, you hit 32 homers," I said. "This year, 10. Why do you think that is?"

Unlike his unfiltered dad, Ike thinks his way around a question before opening his mouth. "Here's what I think," he said. "I've got 10 homers in a little over 300 at-bats. That's not far off a

20-homer pace if I had more at-bats. And it's harder to hit consistently if you're a platoon player. You don't see role players hitting 30 home runs. Could I be doing better? Yeah. Could I have 16 homers instead of 10? Maybe. But you can't keep your pace up playing part time. At least *I* can't."

Did that mean his slumps were his teams' fault?

"No. I haven't played well enough to deserve 600 ABs. But I think I've been decently productive. I went into this season with a goal, a plan to have better at-bats. I wanted to have the same number of strikeouts as walks. I'm close this year, and you know what? I'm proud of that."

As we spoke, he sat in the visitors' clubhouse at Philadelphia's Citizens Bank Park with 67 strikeouts and 60 walks in 325 at-bats to go with those 10 homers. I said it was an unusual goal for a power hitter.

"Striking out is . . . I don't know how to put it. Unfulfilling," Ike said. "It sucks. If you make contact, at least you've got a chance. So that's what I've been trying to do."

"That sounds like the Mets talking."

He laughed. "I want to get better, that's all. I feel like I've given a good effort, but I can do more than I've shown. I've had some weird stuff happen."

"Valley fever," I said, "the ankle problem, the mismanaged Mets . . ."

"I'm only twenty-seven. Not the youngest guy around anymore, but a lot of players don't reach the big leagues till they're twenty-seven. And this season's not over yet. We're in a pennant race, which is as fun as baseball gets. Every game matters, and who knows, you might see me in the World Series."

Two weeks later, with five games remaining in the regular season, Pittsburgh closed to within a game and a half of St. Louis in the NL Central. Ike was with the Pirates in Atlanta, where a chilly breeze had pitchers wearing windbreakers.

At that moment, thermometers back in Scottsdale read 102. "Warmish," Ron called the weather as he hunted baseballs beyond the outfield fences at the Rockies and Diamondbacks' practice fields. "But it's worth it. I'm out here picking up money." Rubbing up a good-as-new ball he'd rescued, he handed it to me. Its hide was smooth and taut. Its feel reminded me that nothing is more tangible and more abstract than a base-ball. It's a fastball, curve, slider, changeup, screwball, splitter, or slurve, depending on its motion; heat or junk, depending on its speed; a ball or strike, depending on the umpire. At the same time, it's nothing but a five-ounce bundle of twine. To make a baseball, you start with a cork sphere the size of a cherry—the "pill" that gives the ball one of its nicknames. Wrap the cork pill in two layers of rubber, then wrap that in a quarter mile of tightly wound yarn. Coat the whole thing in rubber cement. Cover it with two hourglass-shaped strips of leather (horsehide until 1974, alum-tanned American Holstein cowhide since) and sew it up tight with 216 stitches of waxed red thread. Every 2014 major-league baseball was hand-sewn in Rawlings's factory in Turrialba, Costa Rica, where workers earned about fifty-five dollars a week. The result was a bright white, almost perfectly round baseball bearing the signature of Commissioner Allan H. Selig, whose 2014 salary of $18.4 million amounted to $353,846 a week. (Here are the annual salaries of baseball commissioners from 1984 to 2014: Peter Ueberroth, $450,000; Bart Giamatti, $650,000; Fay Vincent, $750,000; Bud Selig, $18.4 million.)

Within minutes, Ron hunted up nine big-league balls worth a total of $171. He drove home whistling.

Ike made a lot more that day: he earned $21,604.94 for that night's Braves–Pirates game without entering the game. He sat on the bench for nine innings, cheering his teammates as they clinched a playoff berth, then joined them in the clubhouse, where the Pirates sprayed each other with beer and champagne.

His father spent the next afternoon putting his travel-team Scottsdale Sidewinders through their paces. Ron smacked a sharp grounder between shortstop and third. Fourteen-year-old Riley Barrett, the .400 hitter with the genius IQ, ranged into the hole for the ball. With no play at first base, he flipped it behind his back to third. Just showin' off. Riley was at short because Jesse, one of Davis's best players, had quit the team. "His dad said he could play," Ron explained. "His mom said he couldn't." Ron had tried to play peace-maker, but it wasn't working, and now he fretted about the boy's baseball future. Jesse's mother said she'd let him go out for his high school team, "but that's almost a handicap," Ron said. Even in prosperous Scottsdale, high school players weren't all that far ahead of the South Phoenix kids the Sidewinders fattened up on. "Compared to us, high schoolers hardly ever practice. Their season is eight games long. My kids play a hundred games a year. Who do you think has more of a chance to max out?"

At home, Ron followed the Pirates online or listened to their games on satellite radio. A week before, he had celebrated when Ike slugged a three-run homer to help Pittsburgh beat the Red Sox. But that night's *Got him, daddy-o* text turned out to be the only one to hit Ron's phone all month. Meanwhile, other baseball dads were sweating out other results. In Phoenix, Diamond-backs TV voice Bob Brenly, who had led the D-backs to victory in the 2001 World Series, called the action at Chase Field while sneaking online peeks at his son Michael's games for the Double-A Portland Sea Dogs. Dan Haren Sr. followed the Dodgers on MLB TV, living and dying with ball-and-strike calls as his son fought to stay in manager Don Mattingly's starting rotation. "I'll call him right away if he wins," Dan Sr. said, "but not if he has a bad outing. Danny's been taking the bad ones pretty hard." After a loss, Dan Sr. let a couple days pass before he called.

IKE DAVIS FINISHED THE REGULAR SEASON with 11 homers, 51 RBIs, and a batting average of .233. He didn't need to be reminded that his numbers looked puny compared to those of Duda, the first baseman the Mets kept when they shipped Ike to Pittsburgh. Duda finished with 30 home runs, the most by a Met since Ike Davis in 2012.

Ike told me he was "feeling good, totally upbeat." While the Mets finished under .500 for the sixth time in a row, he and the Pirates were on their way to the postseason, where one swing can turn around a year, a career, even a life. Just ask Don Larsen, Bill Mazeroski, or Aaron Boone. "When every game really matters, the game's more fun."

Ron, sporting a Pirates cap at Cholla Park, told his Sidewinders they might get to throw a football around with Ike pretty soon. "But not too soon. Not till the Pirates win it all!"

After practice, Ron stowed his gear in his truck, all but a white plastic ball bucket. He flipped the bucket upside down and sat on it, looking past the ball field to the sawtooth skyline of the McDowell Mountains, reflecting on Ike's up-and-down career. He still thought the Mets had screwed up their first-base situation, though their bungling turned out to be a blessing. Getting traded stung Ike's ego, but the Pirates gave him a new start. Too bad he didn't capitalize. Ron thought Ike had seemed to get tentative at the plate. "Sometimes you gotta cut loose, pick one out and give it a rip," he said. "But it's not too late." A homer or two in the playoffs could improve Ike's prospects for 2015. The small-market Pirates' recent success would test their budget. MVP candidate McCutchen, closer Mark Melancon, .315-hitting Josh Harrison, and others would be due for big raises. Russell Martin, the veteran catcher who mentored an improving pitching staff, would be a free agent; it would take more than his current $8.5 million a year to keep Martin in Pittsburgh. Even the injured Álvarez would command double Ike's $3.5 million salary. Despite his enigmatic history, Ike might be a potential bargain for 2015, slightly bruised goods with an upside—proven power—at a time when nothing in baseball was harder to find.

"He'll find a place to play," Ron said. Still, I

wondered if that was what the two of them had in mind when they wrestled with the same choice that decided Babe Ruth's future: pitcher or hitter. Ike had wanted to play every day. It looked like the right decision when he reached the majors at age twenty-three and whacked 32 home runs two seasons later. Was it still the right decision? There was no going back, not with his upper-deck power intact, not with his potential for a 30- or 40-homer season as soon as next year. But he might never shake the platoon-player label. Maybe he should have pitched instead. Or maybe the game was in the process of screwing him. Run out of New York the way Ron had been booed out of Minnesota, pigeon-holed in Pittsburgh, Ike might have been to the mountaintop already, with nothing but a downhill slide ahead.

I asked Ron if he worried about that. We talked about other talented guys who deserved a shot and never got one, or got fouled up by minor-league managers or position coaches, or got reputations they didn't deserve. We talked about guys who got their shot, only to slump or get hurt at the wrong moment, and you never heard their names again. Now it looked like Ike might be one of the snake-bitten ones whose chance slips away.

I asked, "Are you disappointed?"

"Nope." Ron spat tobacco juice into a paper

cup. "He's a star to me. To me, Isaac could wind up a fringe player, a pinch hitter waiting for a few ABs falling off the table. But you know what? Isaac could have played one Little League game and I'd be proud of him. And look at what he's done. He made the high school varsity. That's pretty doggone successful! He was a standout player on a nationally ranked college team, and then a major leaguer. Never mind 32 home runs. He made the big leagues! That makes you a lot better than one in a million."

I hadn't made myself clear. "I meant the game. Has it been unfair to Ike? Are you disappointed in the game?"

Ron shook his head. "It's the best game. I'll tell you the one thing I never liked about fans—when a player's name comes up, they'll ask you, 'Was he any good?' And I'm thinking, 'Well, what do you think? He made the major leagues!' To me, there's three kinds of big-league ballplayer: great, greater, and greatest. We'll have to see where Isaac fits in. And we're in there together, him and me, the 197th father-son combo, and how are you going to beat that?"

13

Two Pennants ★ and a Funeral ★

BOOKIES AND COOKS

For Father's Day 1995, Dad sent me a picture book. The book showed ballplayers in various action poses. On each page, he had pasted a photo of baby Cal's face—blond hair, chubby cheeks—over the player's face. I thought my little boy looked particularly sharp on the pivot of a double play, and his pacifier had to be better than chewing tobacco.

"Don't push him to play," Dad said during one of our evening phone calls.

"I won't."

"Because that's how dads ruin it. He might want to play soccer," he said, making soccer sound like a disease. But he couldn't help asking, "Can he hold a ball yet?"

I knew what he was getting at. "We don't know if he's left-handed yet. But we're hoping."

Dad liked that. "What have you got for the Dads? I'm in second place."

"I'll call you tomorrow."

And then he was gone.

The next day, the phone rang in the Huntington Beach bungalow where Pamela and I lived with two-year-old Cal. Ten p.m. in Indy. It was just getting dark in California.

"Your dad was in an accident," my mother said. He'd been crossing a busy street in the dark, in the rain. A car hit him, knocked him twenty feet, and sped away. A hit-and-run.

"Is he okay? How bad is it?"

"Kevin, he died."

We flew to Indiana. The police had caught the hit-and-run driver, an uninsured kid. They let him go without so much as a traffic ticket because Dad was crossing the street in the middle of the block. Now Cal crawled around the carpet at a funeral home where more than two hundred of Art Cook's friends and fans gathered to mourn his passing. Pamela, who had played a pivotal role in his late-life rally, read my *Sports Illustrated* column about him. His Indy buddies wept. Then it was my turn to speak. All I could think of was how much I wanted to pick up the phone and call him.

I tried to come up with something positive to say. It felt like an act at first, but after a while I could imagine Dad telling me to "give 'em something nice" to think about when they thought of Art "Lefty" Cook.

Standing by his casket, I told his friends, family, and fans that he'd been slipping lately and he knew it. Forgetting things. Repeating himself. Sometimes he talked about visiting old friends in nursing homes, men in their seventies who seemed even older. Some remembered him, some didn't. Some had forgotten who they used to be. "He didn't want to go down that road," I said, "and as it turns out, he didn't. As hard as it is to deal with the shock of how his life ended, I've been thinking there are worse endings. Sad, excruciating deaths that go on for years. But that's not how Dad went out. This way, it's almost like he stepped off the field into the dugout: goodbye."

WITH ROOKIE ACE HIDEO NOMO LEADING THE WAY, the Indy East Dads won a posthumous pennant for him that season.

I spent the next spring training and long stretches of 1996 at ballgames, in clubhouses and press boxes, wondering what Dad would have thought of the first season he missed. Mike Piazza batted .336 and Tony Gwynn .353 that year, while Álex Rodríguez, twenty years old, hit .358 with 36 homers for Seattle. Postgame spreads now featured lobster, grilled vegetables, and mango-glazed salmon. The surprising Yankees, with rookies Derek Jeter and Andy Pettitte, outlasted Greg Maddux, Tom Glavine, and the Braves to win their first World Series since 1978.

A couple years later, we moved to New York, where I went to work at *Sports Illustrated*. That was the season of the record-breaking Mark McGwire–Sammy Sosa home-run chase. Despite suspicions about steroids, the magazine celebrated what it called the sluggers' "Homeric Odyssey" and named them 1998's Sportsmen of the Year. I didn't object—not because I agreed that McGwire and Sosa were "saving baseball," as the magazine had it, but because I saw drug testing as a labor–management issue, a bargaining chip. To get the players' union to agree to testing, I thought, the owners should give up something. A boost in the minimum salary, maybe, or a bigger cut of TV revenue. That's the way the labor–management game was played.

I was wrong. The issue meant more than hairsplitting over arbitration eligibility. Steroids and other performance-enhancing drugs posed an existential threat to the game, and not only because McGwire and Sosa cheated. Their cheating pressured—you could almost say *forced*—other players to cheat too, or be left behind in the race toward 70 home runs. Even today, I can't look at Mark McGwire without thinking that his cheating helped ruin the career of the best player of our time, Barry Bonds, not to mention countless college and high school players who have risked their futures by bulking up chemically, and those who still do. Today, Sosa is a pariah. Bonds has spent several years working his way back to an occasional, informal role with the Giants.

McGwire is the Dodgers' batting coach.

One day, *SI* was photographing McGwire's 70th home-run ball. Comic-book mogul Todd McFarlane, creator of *Spawn*, had paid $3 million for the ball, which arrived at the Time & Life Building in midtown Manhattan with an armed escort. I held it for a few seconds, contemplating the hidden-ball trick.

The $3 million McGwire ball was my second-favorite baseball. My favorite, a gift from an Orioles infielder, was inscribed TO CAL, BEST WISHES FROM CAL RIPKEN JR. PS: NICE NAME!!

Dad would have liked hearing about McGwire and Ripken. He would have loved hearing a story going around the office at the time, a never-reported sequel to *SI*'s 1998 Sportsmen of the Year article: as a condition of flying to New York for a photo shoot with McGwire, Sammy Sosa demanded a private flight home to the Dominican Republic. After the photo shoot, Sosa and his entourage commandeered the plane. They hired a pilot and flew *SI*'s jet around the Caribbean for several days, partying, before ditching it on an airstrip in Santo Domingo. *SI*'s parent company, Time Inc., had to dispatch a pilot to fly the plane home.

BY 2001, I was working part time for MLB Radio, talking baseball with Billy Sample, Seth Everett, and other hosts. Cal, now a Little Leaguer, wore number 2 in honor of his hometown hero, Jeter. His manager happened to be Roger Clemens's dentist. The man shrugged when I called Clemens a headhunter. "Maybe he is," he said, "but you want tough? I did some work on Roger. He was worried about testing positive for drugs, so he wouldn't let me use any anesthetic. He just clenched his fists while I pulled two of his teeth."

Cal's team played in our downtown neighborhood, on a field two blocks from the World Trade Center. He and his little sister, Lily, and I used to ride the ear-popping elevators to the observation deck on the South Tower's 107th floor and look down at his Little League diamond.

On the morning of September 11, I jogged past the towers. Minutes later, the sidewalk shivered. The sound came next, a dull thunder. I looked up to see a gash in the North Tower, smoke pouring out. People hurried into the streets to see what had happened. We thought it was an awful accident. Pamela and four-year-old Lily were home in our apartment five blocks from the towers. Soon I was standing outside with Lily on my shoulders. When the second plane struck the South Tower, sending a fireball through the building toward us, everyone knew this was no accident. It was an attack. Third-grader Cal was across town at the United Nations school. I put his Razor scooter under my arm and took off running.

Cal was pleased to get out of school early. "What's happening?"

"You won't believe it. The towers are on fire."

I kept telling him we'd see them on our way home, but the towers were gone. The more corners we turned, heading downtown, the more barricades we encountered. The police were letting people go north, but not south. "Turn around," a cop would tell us, blocking the way. We'd slip past when he wasn't looking.

Cal asked, "Will the Yankees play tonight?"

"Not tonight," I said, thinking, *not for a while.*

Every surface in our neighborhood—streets, cars, awnings—was shrouded in ash. We were twenty yards from home when a policewoman put her hand on my chest. "Nobody goes that way," she said.

I pointed. "That's our door. My wife and daughter are in there." She let us pass.

Pamela was holding Lily when we rushed in. She'd packed a suitcase with clothes, toys, books, passports, Cal's glove, and a ball. There wasn't time to talk; later, she would describe the awful sound of the towers' falling and the wave of white dust that covered our windows. The four of us walked uptown, shoulder to shoulder with hundreds of others, and spent the night with friends.

There was no baseball for ten days after 9/11. On the twenty-first, when the major leagues resumed play, the Mets' Piazza hit a dramatic home run to beat the Braves. I next saw Piazza and Mets closer John Franco among the emergency workers at the ruins of what was now called Ground Zero. By then, we were living in a furnished apartment in Midtown. Cal played a Little League season on a temporary field while the city used the downtown diamond as a staging area for dump trucks hauling debris from Ground Zero to barges moored in the Hudson.

Two years later, Piazza and Franco dedicated a new diamond on the site of the old one. Franco's son, J.J., joined the dentist's sons as a teammate of Cal's. At first, it was strange to see them running around the same grassy space where they'd played before disaster struck, to look up and see empty sky where the towers had been, but throwing a ball with Cal helped bridge the gap between before and after. Families returned to the Down-town Little League diamond to see Cal's team win the league's first post-9/11 pennant. What the kids liked most, though, was goofing around on their new field between games, trying to make circus catches on fungoes to the outfield fence. Blond, skinny Cal was tireless in the outfield. He'd come home from school, grab my gear bag full of bats and balls, and drag me to the park to play a fantasy game he had invented. Using a lineup drawn from my Rotisserie League team (after joining *SI* I had taken over a franchise from one of the founders), I'd smack long fungoes and narrate the action: "Biggio connects—it's a rocket to the gap! Cal Cook back, back, warning track, wall . . . and he's got it! You're going to see that one on *SportsCenter*!"

On assignment to interview Piazza, I called Cal to let him know how pleasant and mild-mannered the Mets catcher was. "We talked for two hours, and when we got done he said he had nowhere to go, so we had a couple beers. Did you know he was a sixty-second-round draft choice? He remembered his dad, Vince, building a batting cage in their backyard. Mike used to hit in the snow. His dad fired up the barbecue and heated coals to warm Mike's batting gloves." I didn't tell my eleven-year-old the newsy parts of my talks with Piazza: his denying rumors that he was gay, mentioning that he was sleeping with a *Playboy* Playmate I'd once interviewed, and his praise for a supplement containing ephedra—"Ripped Fuel is kind of cool"—a quote that added to the PED whispers that would keep Piazza out of the Hall of Fame in his first two years of eligibility.

I did give my son the gory details of a talk with Curt Schilling after Schilling's "bloody sock" heroics in the 2004 World Series. What fifth-grade boy wouldn't love such a Frankenstein story? Schilling's ankle was shot. He later introduced me to surgeon Bill Morgan, who had grafted a cadaver's tendon into Schilling's foot that fall. The graft leaked blood, creating the ultimate red sock as Schilling and the Sox hearsed the Curse of the Bambino in the 100th World Series. Cal's favorite detail was how Morgan tested the tendon before grafting it into Schilling's ankle.

"He took a piece of a dead guy's foot and just *yanked* it around? Gross!" he said.

Cal took the mound himself in his last summer in the Downtown Little League. Warming him up, I used a phrase from the 1960s, when Dad warmed me up. "Pour it in here." And he did. On his best day on the mound near Ground Zero, twelve-year-old Cal poured fastballs and the occasional changeup past the unbeaten first-place Cubs. The Cubs' pitcher, one of those man-sized Little Leaguers with several no-hitters to his credit, stood almost six feet tall. Nobody gave Cal and his team a chance until they turned a couple of walks, a stolen base, and a ground ball into a 1–0 victory. He was the day's hero.

I told him I was proud of him. He said was just glad the other pitcher didn't hit a liner up the middle. "That guy could hurt somebody."

LIKE HIS GRANDDAD, young Cal liked to bet on ballgames. A dollar of his allowance on the Yanks, a roll of Mentos on the Knicks. That bug must have skipped a generation, because I never caught it. To me, losing ten dollars always felt worse than winning fifteen felt good. But Cal liked a little action.

He was in middle school when I flew to Las Vegas to write about boxer Floyd Mayweather. The welterweight champ, a crazed sports gambler, carried a fanny pack jammed with $30,000 in hundred-dollar bills. I called home to tell Cal that "Money" Mayweather bummed a dollar from me to buy a Snapple, since the vending machine at his gym didn't take hundreds. "Funny story, Dad," Cal said. Then he switched to more important matters. "Since you're in Vegas, will you make a bet for me?"

I had to think about that. I discussed it with his mother. Should we let our son bet on baseball? Well, he'd saved his allowance. He'd studied betting lines like an arbitrageur. We decided to let him invest.

"Who do you like?" I felt like I was twelve again, taking down bets for Dad.

"Dodgers and the over."

"I'm going to feel lousy if you lose your allowance money."

"It's okay if I lose," he said. "It's a good bet." That sounded like wisdom to me.

He won almost a hundred dollars. After that, Cal kept his hand in with occasional small sports bets with his friends. Sometimes I'd get a hunch about a World Series or Super Bowl and offer to back it up with a twenty, but he wouldn't gamble with me. "I don't want to take your money, Dad."

As the years passed and my team, the Bookies, failed to win the original Rotisserie League, Cal took a bigger role in our annual draft. The other guys saw him once a year, on draft day; to them, he seemed to grow up in time-lapse photography, suddenly appearing one April with whiskers on his chin. "He's making me feel old!" said fantasy founding father Peter Gethers. I said he was starting to make me feel short.

Between drafts, Cal crunched numbers and ranked players according to newer stats like batting average on balls in play (BABIP) and defense-independent pitching statistics (DIPS) while I stuck to batting average and RBIs—until he convinced me that the new metrics could help predict batting average, homers, RBIs, wins, ERA, and the other old reliables that win and lose fantasy pennants. A hitter with a .350 BABIP, for example, is bound to lose batting average the next year—because he got lucky. When a batter puts a ball in play, it typically falls safely about three-tenths of the time, so you should expect anyone with a BABIP over .300 to lose batting average the following year. On the other hand, unlucky pitchers who allow a BABIP over .300 tend to improve the next year. Such stats have spawned other, more specialized metrics as major-league teams, gamblers, and fantasy league players deploy more sophisticated numbers every year.

Twenty years ago, Tony La Russa was humored as a "stats geek" for studying computer readouts on hitters' tendencies. In Game Seven of the 2014 World Series, with the tying run at second and the Giants' Madison Bumgarner on the mound, the Royals' Nori Aoki sliced a season-saving double to left. Except that it wasn't a double. Left fielder Juan Pérez was practically standing on the left-field line. Perfectly positioned in the Giants' outfield defense, shifted leftward according to an algorithm that paired Bumgarner and Aoki's tendencies as if they were chromosomes of the next play's DNA, Pérez snagged the line drive that would have tied Game Seven. To paraphrase Russ Hodges, "The metrics win the pennant!"

I think fantasy baseball has helped save baseball. Throughout the 1970s and '80s, the game lost ground to NFL football, but baseball rallied, thanks in no small part to more than twelve million fantasy players who might have ignored the game if not for the skin they had in it. When Cal went to college at Syracuse, he parlayed his sports-betting and Rotisserie experience into an occasionally lucrative hobby. He plays fantasy sports at FanDuel.com and DraftKings.com, competing with other young gamblers, sometimes thousands of them at a time. The best thing about those daily or weekly betting pools is that he can stay even or make a few dollars simply by beating half the participants.

For him, that's like Rocks for Jocks 101. The worst thing about FanDuel-type contests is that there are sharks in the pool, experts who earn a living at it. But Cal competes. In September 2014, he spent his last virtual cent on Pirates shortstop Jordy Mercer, who homered to win Cal $500. He came in third out of 6,295 in that day's contest.

"Good going," I said. "Should the Bookies get Jordy?"

"No, Jimmy Rollins is better."

"Well, what have you got for the Bookies? We've got free-agent bidding on Sunday."

With Cal at Syracuse, we now had our own Dad Reports. He'd give me his take on ballplayers. "Volquez is getting lucky. We should pick up Drew Storen. I still like Ike, but he's not playing enough." I'd give him updates on my work. "Dee Gordon's mom got murdered when he was six. His dad, Tom 'Flash' Gordon, raised him while pitching for eight big-league teams. Bob Boone's in the Nationals' front office now. He says they want all their young pitchers to have Tommy John surgery, just to get it over with. He's joking."

Sometimes there wasn't much sports news, so we'd keep it short. My end of the call wouldn't be much more than "Hi Cal, bla bla, Mike Trout, bla bla, do you believe what Girardi did? Kershaw 15 Ks! Okay, goodnight, I love you." When Dad and I spoke, the *I love you* part was subtext. A generation later, we come right out and say it.

As the 2014 season wound down, our Bookies were in the tightest pennant race in Rotisserie League history. With two weeks left, five of the league's ten teams were still in the hunt. We jockeyed for position, riding Drew Storen's saves to a crucial point in that category, only to lose points in ERA and WHIP when the Diamondbacks' Wade Miley did his best impression of the old-time Reds' scattershot Billy McCool. With a week to go, we were half a point out of first.

"We've got to dump Miley," I said one night. "Dan Haren's available."

"He's scary," Cal said. "That's why he's available."

I argued that Haren looked better than his numbers. He had two home starts coming up. He was generally stingy with base runners. Cal pointed to Haren's 4.14 ERA. Haren had allowed more hits than innings pitched, and twenty-six of those hits were round-trippers. "You like him because he's in your book," Cal said. "Maybe he's a great guy, but there's no category for that. He was terrible for the Nationals last year."

"He was lonesome! He missed his family." I kept pushing for Haren. "How much can he hurt us?" But Cal hated his metrics. "He doesn't miss enough bats." That was true: Haren was striking out fewer batters than ever. "And he gives up too many homers." Maybe so, I said, but the guy was a gamer. "He's pitching for his career." I kept at it until Cal gave me his blessing.

A couple nights later, with the Dodgers trying to clinch the National League West and the Rotisserie pennant on the line, Haren took the mound against second-place San Francisco. Gregor Blanco, the Giants' leadoff man, promptly crushed a homer to center. I was following the action on ESPN.com, where the Gamecast feature showed the ball as a blue dart over a pixellated crowd in the center-field seats. The Rotisserie race was so close that Blanco's home run and a handful of other darts sent the Bookies from first to third place in a matter of minutes.

Then Haren settled down. He escaped the first inning with no further damage. In fact, he responded to Blanco's homer with seven no-hit innings. Five days later, Haren had another solid start against the Rockies. His strong finish was worth $10 million to him—by reaching 180 innings pitched, he qualified for the option that would earn him the same salary in 2015. Almost as important to Haren, he'd be able to stay in Los Angeles for another year. (Or so he thought.) Meanwhile, his teammate Adrián González went on a final-week homer binge, the Nats' Jordan Zimmermann spun a final-day no-hitter, and my phone buzzed on the season's last day.

A text from Cal: *Bookies win!*

I texted back: *Lets celebrate. A road trip?*

EPILOGUE
★ *Home of the Ponies* ★

At the end of October, I drove north to Syracuse with a couple of sandwiches, a duffel bag, and a map. Driving through New Jersey and the Delaware Water Gap in a cold rain, I thought back to the season's end and a month's worth of playoffs.

Both batting titles had come down to the final day. In the American League, Houston's pint-sized José Altuve could have preserved his three-point edge by taking the day off. Astros manager Tom Lawless left him out of the lineup, but Altuve insisted on playing, then went two-for-four to claim the crown the right way. "If you want to win something, you should win it on the field," he said. The Rockies' Justin Morneau backed into the National League batting title by sitting out the last two games, then grounding out in a meaningless at-bat after his lead on the Pirates' Josh Harrison was safe. The Rockies would keep Morneau in 2015; the Bookies would not.

Pittsburgh faced the Giants in the NL Wild Card Game, nine innings to determine who would meet Washington in the Division Series, which would decide who advanced to the League

Championship Series, which would in turn decide who reached the World Series. All those rounds of playoffs cheapened the regular season but maximized revenue. The Angels, Orioles, Nationals, and Dodgers had proved they were the year's best teams, but their seasons amounted to an out-of-town preview for the playoffs.

Ike Davis hoped to redeem his season in the playoffs, starting with the Wild Card Game, but with left-hander Madison Bumgarner pitching for the Giants, he spent the game nailed to the bench. Ike kept his stubbly chin up as Bumgarner beat Pirates starter Edinson Volquez, 8–0. Three hours and twelve minutes into the postseason, Ike now had an official line of postseason stats, all zeroes.

"I was a tougher out this year," he said before flying home to Arizona. "Maybe that's something to build on." The Pirates soon traded him to Oakland—a new chance for Ike in 2015.

Dan Haren, whose Dodgers won the NL West but lost the Division Series to St. Louis, drove home to tickle his kids and play full-time dad for five months. The Dodgers soon crossed him up by trading him to the Miami Marlins, leaving Haren to fret about his near future. Should he spend another $10 million season as a mostly absentee dad? Demand another trade? Or retire?

Ron Shelton tweaked the script of a *Bull Durham* musical that was due to hit Broadway in

2015. Barry Bonds, walking on crutches after hip surgery, threw out the first ball before a Giants victory over the Cardinals in the NL Championship Series. Aaron Boone called that game for ESPN Radio.

On the highway between Scranton, Pennsylvania, and Binghamton, New York, towns with rich minor-league histories, I checked in with Aaron's brother. Bret Boone's fifteen-year-old son, Jake, had been working out with the varsity team at San Diego's Torrey Pines High School. At five foot eight and 170 pounds, Jake was growing into the size he'd need to become the game's first fourth-generation major leaguer, and checking his height almost hourly. Bret tried not to push him too hard. "I don't want to be one of those pushy baseball dads," he said. "When I was fifteen, my dad lectured me about getting serious about baseball. I said, 'Dad, there's girls, too. There's parties.' Today, kids take their workouts and diet almost too seriously. I wind up telling Jake, 'Go to football games, have a hot dog. Be a kid!'"

I asked Bret about Aaron's immortal 2003 ALCS homer against the Red Sox. He reminded me of their dad's take on the Boones' greatest postseason moment: as proud as Bob Boone was of Aaron, his competitive streak kicked in when he talked about Aaron's home run.

"That knuckleball from Wakefield didn't

knuckle," Bob told me. "I mean, hell, *I* could have hit that ball out."

Bret disagreed. "Dad didn't have Aaron's power. I'm saying warning track for Dad, *maybe*."

Next, I called another ballplayer's child. Julia Ruth Stevens, eighty-three years older than Jake Boone, had been disappointed by the auction of the Babe's watch. While Ruthian bats and jerseys sold for millions, she and son Tom had settled for $650,000 for the watch, a hefty sum that was less than they'd hoped for. Not enough, after taxes, to pay off a granddaughter's student loans and cover the Stevenses' move to Hawaii. "I may not go to Hawaii after all, but it's all right," Julia told me. "I've got my memories." She hoped to throw out a few more ceremonial first pitches in 2015, the year she turns ninety-nine. "I'm actually throwing better now. Here's my secret: every time, I stand a little closer to the catcher."

A COUPLE HOURS LATER, I pulled up at the house where Cal lived off-campus. "Hey Dad," he said, hopping into the passenger seat. We drove north to Watertown, New York, another town with a creaky baseball history. From there, it was half an hour to the Canadian border. Cal spent a minute filling me in on his classes. Since there wasn't much 2014 baseball left, we spent the rest of the time talking about his FanDuel NFL choices, aided by an NFL.com feature called Coach's Film, which allows anyone to study every play of every game from various angles in slow motion as if he were Peyton Manning.

At the border, we drove over the Thousand Islands Bridge. I pictured Dad going over this bridge on a team bus, looking down at the same wooded islands in the St. Lawrence River. I talked about playing backyard baseball with Dad, and how he used to do good deeds that nobody noticed. If he had a few extra dollars, he'd drive your car to the gas station, fill it up, and bring it back without saying a word. I quoted his countrified sayings: "That fence is cattywampus" and "Oh, for cryin' in a bucket."

Cal said, "You've told me that stuff a million times." I must have looked crestfallen. He added, "They're good stories, though."

Driving west to Kingston, I asked myself why baseball mattered. Maybe it didn't. Or maybe it stitched us together, giving us something to share, if only to pass the time on the phone, another way to say, "I love you." And maybe baseball serves to stop time in our memories. As every fan with a philosophic bent will tell you, the game exists outside time, clockless. Baseball memories, from Babe Ruth's swing to Madison Bumgarner's high fastballs in the 2014 World Series, seem to inhabit the same timeless space. At least they do to me. The older I get, the more I worry about rushing through life, always hurrying to the next thing, paying too little attention to the better moments of my threescore years.

Yesterday's rain gave way to bright sun. The temperature in Canada was 17, but that was Celsius. My dashboard gauge read 63F as we entered Kingston, Ontario, a pretty town of 120,000 on the northeast shore of Lake Ontario. We pulled into a small, empty parking lot in a neglected part of town called Swamp Ward. Doug Graham, a sixty-four-year-old sportswriter for the *Kingston Whig-Standard*, met us and walked us onto a well-kept field surrounded by chain-link fences.

"This is where your dad played," Graham said. "Of course it looked a lot different then." He described Megaffin Stadium in the late 1940s, with its grandstands, a press box behind the plate, and eight-foot wooden fences in the outfield. "The left-field fence stood in front of those poplars," he said, pointing. Those poplars were about all that remained of Megaffin Stadium, the Border League's jewel of a ballpark, which once held more than 1,500 fans. Now it was Megaffin Park, a municipal facility that hosted high school and college games. Still, its jade-green grass and grainy clay infield were in better shape than a typical American junior-college field. Cal looked around. "Not as fancy as I thought, but I like it," he said.

I lugged my duffel bag to the plate and fished out two gloves and a ball. Cal went to shortstop, I stood at first under a high, cloudless sky. It's easy to forget how big a full-sized field is—he looked a mile away. The first grounder I threw him died in the grass behind the mound. I put some zip on the next one. Soon he was backhanding grounders, gunning strikes to first. The former second baseman for the United Nations school could still pick it.

After a while, he said, "My arm's falling off. I'll catch you."

Graham met me on the mound. He brought a gift: a Kingston Ponies cap like the one Dad wore in 1948, the year he won 21 games. "This place was loved when your dad pitched here," he said. "So was he."

The rest of Megaffin Stadium may be gone, but the mound and the plate still stand on the spots they occupied on Art Cook Appreciation Night sixty-six years ago. Digging my shoe into the dent in front of the rubber, I tried to hear the cheers Art Cook heard that night.

Cal crouched behind the plate, holding his glove out to give me a target. "Pour it in here, Dad," he said.

ACKNOWLEDGMENTS

A book that involves almost a century of baseball needs plenty of help. I've been lucky in that department.

Ron Davis, for starters. An All-Star reliever in his time, Davis was a force throughout my year in and out of his life. He's a good quote and good company. The same goes for Ike, who shared the ups and downs of his 2014 season. Thanks also to Kendall Davis, who provided photos and routed emails between us.

I owe thanks to three generations of Boones. Sharp, opinionated Bob shared his views on our evolving national pastime and put me in touch with his three sons. Bret became my go-to Boone, thoughtful and funny, often irreverent about the game he loves. Aaron brought a middle kid's perspective. His commentary became part of the book as well as the soundtrack of the postseason as my kids and I listened to the 2014 playoffs and World Series on the radio. And while I didn't delve into Matt Boone's too-brief baseball career, Matt helped me understand the family dynamic. Then there was an unexpected perk: finding out about Jake Boone, Bret's fifteen-year-old son, who might become the first fourth-generation big leaguer by 2023.

Julia Ruth Stevens shared her vivid memories of her famous father with me. Tom and Anita Stevens invited me into their home, stayed in touch throughout the season, and helped me feel connected to baseball's First Family.

Doug Graham of the *Kingston Whig-Standard* welcomed Cal and me to Dad's favorite Canadian town. Doug showed us around Megaffin Park, where Dad pitched sixty-six years ago, and gave me a Kingston Ponies cap that's priceless to me. Tom Carty dug up faded clippings from Art Cook's best years and threw a ball around with Cal and me. I'm glad to have friends in Kingston like Doug and Tom. Readers who want to follow the 2015 Ponies should check out http://www.kingstonponies.com.

In Cooperstown, senior curator Tom Shieber and media director Craig Muder welcomed me to the Hall of Fame. Emily Bayci provided invaluable assistance with my research.

At Norton, Tom Mayer's a friend as well as the best editor in town. If editors had a BABIP stat (batting average on books in print?), he'd be hitting a thousand. Bill Rusin's advice and support were essential as ever. Ryan Harrington, an invaluable teammate, came through again and again on my behalf. Ingsu Liu and her designers produced a superb jacket, and publicist Lauren Opper helped get the book out in the world.

Many thanks also to Don Rifkin, Laura Goldin, and Steve Colca.

Patricia Cook's support was crucial at every turn. Generous with her time, her recollections and more, she came through with whatever I needed. Thanks, Mom.

In different ways, Dan Haren Jr. and Sr., Ron Shelton, Dusty Baker, and economist David Laband made major contributions. They became friends of the book. I learned a lot about the game from Barry Bonds, the late Bobby Bonds, Curt Schilling, Michael Jordan, Al Rosen, Donald Fehr, Cal Ripken Jr., and the late Tony Gwynn. I'm also grateful, for various important reasons, to Tom Gordon, Bob Brenly, Kate Nolan, Steve Madey and the Miracle Leaguers of Westchester County, Fred Lynn, Pete Rose, Mark Frost, Joie Casey, David Powell, Walter and Chase Sadowski, Don Megaffin, Randy Phillips, Mike Vaccaro, Liz Halsted and David Barnes, Barry Meister, Jack Hamilton, Pat Neshek, Jeff Long, John Hines, Jay Horwitz, John Rezek, Steve Randall, Jenny Llakmani, Barbara Nellis, Helen Rosenberg, ESPN's Kristen Hudek and Allison Stoneberg, and Christina Carter.

No book of mine is complete without a nod to Ken Kubik, guru of New Jersey's Grass Roots Turf Products, and our fellow members of Ken's contingent, Babe Ruth expert Doug Vogel and Kubik Klassic sandbagger Chris Carson.

At home, I rely on Pamela Marin, whose superb *Motherland* is this book's partner. Dad would also want me to thank Calloway Marin Cook and Lily Lady Cook. Both contributed to *The Dad Report*. To use one of Dad's terms, he would have been tickled to know them.

SELECT BIBLIOGRAPHY

Angell, Roger. *Five Seasons: A Baseball Companion*. New York: Simon and Schuster, 1977.

Berkow, Ira. *Summers at Shea*. Chicago: Triumph Books, 2013.

Bouton, Jim. *Ball Four*. New York: Dell, 1971.

Bryan, Mike. *Baseball Lives*. New York: Pantheon Books, 1989.

Canseco, José. *Juiced*. New York: William Morrow, 2005.

Castro, Tony. *Mickey Mantle: America's Prodigal Son*. Dulles, VA: Potomac Books, 2002.

Creamer, Robert W. *Babe*. New York: Simon and Schuster, 1974.

Fainaru-Wada, Mark, and Lance Williams. *Game of Shadows*. New York: Gotham Books, 2006.

Hirsch, James S. *Willie Mays: The Life, the Legend*. New York: Scribner, 2009.

Honig, Donald. *Baseball Between the Lines: Baseball in the Forties and Fifties, as Told by the Men Who Played It*. Lincoln, NE: University of Nebraska Press, 1993.

—. *Baseball When the Grass Was Real*. Lincoln, NE: Bison Books, 1993.

James, Bill. *The Bill James Baseball Abstract*. New York: Ballantine Books, 1982–1988.

—. *Whatever Happened to the Hall of Fame?* New York: Free Press, 1995.

Jenkinson, Bill. *The Year Babe Ruth Hit 104 Home Runs: Recrowning Baseball's Greatest Slugger*. Boston: Da Capo Press, 2007.

Keri, Jonah. *Baseball Between the Numbers*. New York: Basic Books, 2006.

Lardner, Ring. *Ring Around the Bases*. New York: Charles Scribner's Sons, 1992.

Lazenby, Roland. *Michael Jordan: The Life*. New York: Little, Brown and Company, 2014.

Lewis, Michael. *Moneyball*. New York: W. W. Norton & Company, 2003.

Lyle, Sparky, with Peter Golenbock. *The Bronx Zoo*. New York: Crown, 1979.

Ritter, Lawrence S. *The Babe: A Life in Pictures*. New York: Ticknor & Fields, 1988.

Roth, Philip. *The Great American Novel*. New York: Holt, Rinehart & Winston, 1973.

Sowell, Mike. *The Pitch That Killed*. New York: Macmillan, 1989.

Stevens, Julia Ruth, with Bill Gilbert. *Major League Dad: A Daughter's Cherished Memories*. Chicago: Triumph Books, 2001.

Stoodley, Dave. *Chronicle of the Watertown Athletics and the Border Baseball League, 1946 to 1951*. Adams Center, NY: DCS Sports Publications, 2012.

Updike, John. *Hub Fans Bid Kid Adieu*. New York: The Library of America, 2010.

Vaccaro, Mike. *Emperors and Idiots*. New York: Doubleday, 2005.

Waggoner, Glen, ed. *Rotisserie League Baseball*. New York: Bantam Books, 1984.

Wendel, Tim. *High Heat*. Philadelphia: Da Capo Press, 2010.

Will, George F. *Men at Work: The Craft of Baseball*. New York: Macmillan, 1990.

Center Point Large Print
600 Brooks Road / PO Box 1
Thorndike, ME 04986-0001 USA

(207) 568-3717

US & Canada:
1 800 929-9108
www.centerpointlargeprint.com